Rosa Nouchette Carey

**Not like other Girls**

Vol. I

Rosa Nouchette Carey

**Not like other Girls**
*Vol. I*

ISBN/EAN: 9783337040772

Printed in Europe, USA, Canada, Australia, Japan

Cover: Foto ©ninafisch / pixelio.de

More available books at **www.hansebooks.com**

# NOT LIKE OTHER GIRLS.

A Novel.

BY

ROSA NOUCHETTE CAREY,

AUTHOR OF

'NELLIE'S MEMORIES,' 'BARBARA HEATHCOTE'S TRIAL,'
'MARY ST. JOHN,' ETC.

IN THREE VOLUMES.
VOL. I.

LONDON:
RICHARD BENTLEY AND SON,
Publishers in Ordinary to Her Majesty the Queen.
1884.

# TO MY NIECES.

# CONTENTS OF VOL. I.

| CHAPTER | | PAGE |
|---|---|---|
| I. | FIVE O'CLOCK TEA | 1 |
| II. | DICK OBJECTS TO THE MOUNTAINS | 20 |
| III. | MR. MAYNE MAKES HIMSELF DISAGREEABLE | 40 |
| IV. | DICK'S FÊTE | 58 |
| V. | 'I AM QUITE SURE OF HIM' | 75 |
| VI. | MR. TRINDER'S VISIT | 92 |
| VII. | PHILLIS'S CATECHISM | 111 |
| VIII. | 'WE SHOULD HAVE TO CARRY PARCELS' | 131 |
| IX. | A LONG DAY | 151 |
| X. | THE FRIARY | 167 |
| XI. | 'TELL US ALL ABOUT IT, NAN' | 189 |
| XII. | 'LADDIE' PUTS IN AN APPEARANCE | 211 |
| XIII. | 'I MUST HAVE GRACE' | 228 |
| XIV. | 'YOU CAN DARE TO TELL ME THESE THINGS!' | 250 |
| XV. | A VAN IN THE BRAIDWOOD ROAD | 274 |
| XVI. | A VISIT TO THE WHITE HOUSE | 300 |

# NOT LIKE OTHER GIRLS.

## CHAPTER I.

#### FIVE O'CLOCK TEA.

FIVE o'clock tea was a great institution in Oldfield.

It was a form of refreshment to which the female inhabitants of that delightful place were strongly addicted. In vain did Dr. Weatherby, the great authority in all that concerned the health of the neighbourhood, lift up his voice against the mild feminine dram-drinking of these modern days, denouncing it in no measured terms; the ladies of Oldfield listened incredulously, and, softly quoting Cowper's lines as to the 'cup that cheers and not inebriates,' still presided over their dainty little tea-tables, and vied with each other in the beauty of their china, and the flavour of their highly-scented Pekoe.

In spite of Dr. Weatherby's sneers and innuendoes, a great deal of valuable time was spent in lingering in one or another of the pleasant drawing-rooms of the place. As the magic hour approached, people dropped in casually. The elder ladies sipped their tea and gossiped softly; the younger ones, if it were summer-time, strolled out through the open windows into the garden. Most of the houses had tennis-grounds, and it was quite an understood thing that a game should be played before they separated.

With some few exceptions the inhabitants of Oldfield were wealthy people. Handsome houses standing in their own grounds were dotted here and there among the lanes and country roads. Some of the big houses belonged to very big people indeed; but these were aristocrats who only lived in their country houses a few months in the year, and whose presence added more to the dignity than to the hilarity of the neighbourhood.

With these exceptions, the Oldfield people were highly gregarious and hospitable; in spite of a few peculiarities, they had their good points; a great deal of gossip prevailed, but it was in the main harmless and good-natured. There was a wonderful simplicity of dress, too, which in these days might be termed a cardinal virtue. The girls wore their fresh cambrics and plain straw hats; no one seemed to think it necessary to put on smart clothing when they wished to visit their friends. People said this Arcadian simplicity was just as studied; nevertheless it showed perfection of taste and a just appreciation of things.

The house that was considered the most attractive in Oldfield, and where, on summer afternoons, the sound of youthful voices and laughter were the loudest, was Glen Cottage, a small white house adjoining the long village street, belonging to a certain Mrs. Challoner, who lived here with her three daughters.

This may be accounted strange in the first instance, since the Challoners were people of the most limited income—an income so small that nothing but the most modest of entertainments could be furnished to their friends; very different to their neighbours at Longmead, the large white house adjoining, where sumptuous dinners and regular evening parties were given in the dark days when pleasures were few and tennis impossible.

People said it was very good-natured of the Maynes; but then when there is an only child in the case, an honest, pleasure-loving, gay young fellow, on whom his parents doat, what is it they will not do to please their own flesh and blood; and, as young Richard Mayne—or Dick, as he was always called—loved all such festive gatherings, Mrs. Mayne loved them too; and her husband tried to persuade himself that his tastes lay in the same direction, only reserving certain groans for private use, that Dick could not be happy without a houseful of young people.

But no such entertainments were possible at Glen Cottage; nevertheless the youth of the neighbourhood flocked eagerly into the pleasant drawing-room where Mrs. Challoner sat tranquilly summer and winter to welcome her friends, or betook themselves through the open French windows into the old-fashioned garden, in which mother and daughters took such pride.

On hot afternoons the tea-table was spread under an acacia-tree; low wicker-chairs were brought out, and rugs spread on the lawn; and Nan and her sisters dispensed strawberries and cream, with the delicious home-made bread and butter; while Mrs. Challoner sat among a few chosen spirits knitting and talking in her pleasant low-toned voice, quite content that the burthen of responsibility should rest upon her daughters.

Mrs. Challoner always smiled when people told her that she ought to be proud of her girls. No daughters were ever so much to their mother as hers; she simply lived in and for them; she saw with their eyes, thought with their thoughts—was hardly herself at all, but Nan and Phillis and Dulce, each by turns.

Long ago they had grown up to her growth. Mrs. Challoner's nature was hardly a self-sufficing one. During her husband's lifetime she had been braced by his influence and cheered by his example, and had sought to guide her children according to his directions; in a word, his manly strength had so supported her that no one, not even her shrewd young daughters, guessed at the interior weakness.

When her stay was removed, Mrs. Challoner ceased to guide, and came down to her children's level. She was more like their sister than their mother, people said; and yet no mother was more cherished than she.

Her very weakness made her sacred in her daughters' eyes; her widowhood, and a certain failure of health, made her the subject of their choicest care.

It could not be said that there was much amiss, but years ago a doctor whom Mrs. Challoner had consulted had looked grave, and mentioned the name of a disease of which certain symptoms reminded him. There was no ground for present apprehension; the whole thing was very shadowy and unsubstantial—a mere hint—a question of care; nevertheless the word had been said, and the mischief done.

From that time Mrs. Challoner was wont to speak gloomily of her health, as of one doomed. She was by nature languid and lymphatic, but now her languor increased; always averse to effort, she now left all action to her daughters. It was they who decided and regulated the affairs of their modest household, and rarely were such wise young rulers to be found in girls of their age. Mrs. Challoner merely acquiesced, for in Glen Cottage there was seldom a dissentient voice, unless it were that of Dorothy, who had been Dulce's nurse, and took upon herself the airs of an old servant who could not be replaced.

They were all pretty girls, the three Misses Challoner, but Nan was *par excellence* the prettiest. No one could deny that fact who saw them together. Her features were more regular than her sisters', and her colour more transparent. She was tall, too, and her figure had a certain willowy grace that was most uncommon; but what attracted people most was a frankness and unconsciousness of manner that was perfectly charming.

Phillis, the second sister, was not absolutely pretty, perhaps, but she was nice-looking, and there was something in her expression that made people say she was clever; she could talk on occasions with a fluency that was quite surprising, and that would cast Nan into the shade. 'If I were only as clever as Phillis!' Nan would sigh.

Then there was Dulce, who was only just eighteen, and whom her sisters treated as the family pet; who was light and small and nimble in her movements, and looked even younger than she really was.

Nobody ever noticed if Dulce were pretty; no one questioned if her features were regular or not, or cared to do such a thing. Only when she smiled, the prettiest dimple came into her cheek, and her eyes had a fearless childlike look in them; for the rest, she was just Dulce.

The good-looking daughters of a good-looking mother, as somebody called them; and there was no denying Mrs. Challoner was still wonderfully well-preserved, and in spite of her languor and invalid airs a very pretty woman.

Five o'clock tea had long been over at the cottage this afternoon, and a somewhat lengthy game of tennis had followed; after which the visitors had dispersed as usual, and the girls had come in to prepare for the half-past seven o'clock dinner—for Glen Cottage followed the fashion of its richer neighbours, and set out its frugal meal with a proper accompaniment of flower-vases and evening toilette.

The three sisters came up the lawn together, but Nan carried her racquet a little languidly—she looked a trifle grave.

Mrs. Challoner laid down her knitting and looked at them, and then she regarded her watch plaintively.

'Is it late, mother?' asked Nan, who never missed any of her mother's movements. 'Ten minutes past seven—no wonder the afternoon seemed long.'

'No one found it long but Nan,' observed Dulce, with an arch glance at her sister, at which Nan slightly coloured, but took no further notice. 'By-the-bye,' she continued, as though struck by a sudden recollection, 'what can have become of Dick this afternoon? he so seldom fails us without telling us beforehand.'

'That will soon be explained,' observed Phillis oracularly, as the gate-bell sounded, and was immediately followed by sharp footsteps on the gravel, and the unceremonious entrance of a young man through the open window.

'Better late than never,' exclaimed two of the girls. Nan said, 'Why, what has made you play truant, Dick?' in a slightly injured voice. But Mrs. Challoner merely smiled at him, and said nothing—young men were her natural enemies, and she knew it. She was civil to them and endured their company, and that was all.

Dick Mayne was not a formidable-looking individual; he was a strong, thick-set young fellow, with broad shoulders, not much above middle height, and decidedly plain, except in his mother's eyes; and she thought even Dick's sandy hair beautiful.

But in spite of his plainness he was a pleasant, well-bred young fellow, with a fund of good-humour and drollery, and a pair of honest eyes that people learnt to trust. Everyone liked him, and no one ever said a word in his dispraise; and for the rest, he could tyrannize as royally as any other young man who is his family's sole blessing.

'It was all my ill-luck,' grumbled Dick.

'Trevanion of Exeter came over to our place, and of course the mater pressed him to stay for luncheon; and then nothing would do but a long walk over Hilberry Downs.'

'Why did you not bring him here?' interrupted Dulce, with a pout; 'you tiresome Dick, when you must know what a godsend a strange young man is in these wilds!'

'My dear!' reproved her mother.

'Oh, but it is true, mamma,' persisted the outspoken Dulce. 'Think how pleased Carrie and Sophy Paine would have been at the sight of a fresh face! it was horrid of you, sir!'

'I wanted him to come,' returned the young man, in a deprecating voice. 'I told him how awfully jolly it always is here, and that he would be sure to meet a lot of nice people, but there was no persuading him: he wanted a walk and a talk about our fellows. That is the worst of Trevanion, he always will have his own way.'

'Never mind,' returned Nan pleasantly; she seemed to have recovered her sprightliness all at once. 'It is very good of you to come so often; and we had Mr. Parker and his cousin to look after the Paines.'

'Oh yes! we did very well,' observed Phillis tranquilly. 'Mother, now Dick has come so late, he had better stay.'

'If I only may do so?' returned Dick; but his inquiry was directed to Nan.

'Oh yes, you may stay,' she remarked carelessly, as she moved away; but there was a little pleased smile on her face that he failed to see. She nodded pleasantly to him as he darted forward to open the door. It was Nan who always dispensed the hospitalities of the house, whose decision was unalterable. Dick had learned what it was to be sent about his business; only once had he dared to remain without her sovereign permission, and on that occasion he had been treated by her with such dignified politeness that he would rather have been sent to Coventry.

This evening the fates were propitious, and Dick understood that the sceptre of favour was to be extended to him. When the girls had flitted into the little dusky hall he closed the door, and sat down happily beside Mrs. Challoner, to whom he descanted eloquently of the beauties of Hilberry and the virtues of Ned Trevanion.

Mrs. Challoner listened placidly as the knitting-needles flashed between her long white fingers. She was very fond of Dick, after her temperate fashion; she had known him from a child, and had seen him grow up amongst them until he had become like a son of the house. Dick, who had no brothers and sisters of his own, and whose parents had not married until they were long past youth, had adopted brotherly airs with the Challoner girls; they called each other by their Christian names, and he reposed in them the confidences that young men are wont to give to their belongings.

With Nan this easy familiarity had of late merged into something different: a reserve, a timidity, a subtle suspicion of change had crept into their intimacy. Nan felt that Dick's manner had altered, but somehow she liked it better; his was always a sweet bountiful nature, but now it seemed to have deepened into greater manliness. Dick was growing older; Oxford training was polishing him. After each one of his brief absences Nan saw a greater change, a more marked deference, and secretly hoped that no one else noticed it.

When the young undergraduate wrote dutiful letters home, the longest messages were always for Nan; when he carried little offerings of flowers to his young neighbours, Nan's bouquet was always the choicest; he distinguished her, too, on all occasions by those small nameless attentions which never fail to please.

Nan kept her own counsel, and never spoke of these things. She said openly that Dick was very nice and very much improved, and that they always missed him sadly during the Oxford terms; but she never breathed a syllable that might make people suspect that this very ordinary young man with the sandy hair was more to her than other young men. Nevertheless Phillis and Dulce knew that such was the case, and Mrs. Challoner understood that the most dangerous enemy to her peace was this lively-spoken Dick.

Dick was very amusing, for he was an eloquent young fellow; nevertheless Mrs. Challoner sighed more than once, and her attention visibly wandered; seeing which, Dick good-humouredly left off talking, and began inspecting the different articles in Nan's work-basket.

'I am afraid I have given your mother a headache,' he said, when they were sitting round the circular table in the low, oddly-shaped dining-room. There was a corner cut off, and the windows were in unexpected places, which made it unlike other rooms; but Dick loved it better than the great dining-room at Longmead; and somehow it never had looked cosier to him than it did this evening. It was somewhat dark, owing to the shade of the veranda; so the lamp was lighted, and the pleasant scent of roses and lilies came through the open windows. A belated wasp hovered round the specimen glasses that Nan had filled; Dick tried to make havoc of the enemy with his table-napkin. The girls' white dresses suited their fresh young faces. Nan had fastened a crimson rose in her gown; Phillis and Dulce had knots of blue ribbon. 'Trevanion does not know what he lost by his obstinacy,' thought Dick, as he glanced round the table.

'What were you and the mother discussing?' asked Dulce curiously.

'Dick was telling me about his friend. He seemed a very superior young man,' returned Mrs. Challoner. 'I suppose you have asked him for your party next week?'

Dick turned very red at this question. 'Mater asked him, you may trust her for that. If it were not for father, I think she would turn the whole house out of the windows—every day some one fresh is invited.'

'How delightful! and all in your honour,' exclaimed Dulce mischievously.

'That spoils the whole thing,' grumbled the heir of the Maynes; 'it is a perfect shame that a fellow cannot come of age quietly, without his people making this fuss. I begin to think I was a fool for my pains to refuse the ball.'

'Yes, indeed; just because you were afraid of the supper speeches,' laughed Dulce, 'when we all wanted it so.

'Never mind,' returned Dick sturdily; 'the mater shall give us one in the winter, and we will have Godfrey's band, and I will get all our fellows to come.'

'That will be delightful,' observed Nan, and her eyes sparkled—already she saw herself led out for the first dance by the son of the house—but Dulce interrupted her.

'But all the same I wish Dick had not been so stupid about it. No one knows what may happen before the winter. I hate put-off things.'

'A bird in the hand is worth two in the bush—eh, Miss Dulce?'

'Yes; indeed, that proverb is truer than people think,' she replied, with a wise nod of her head. 'Don't you remember, Nan, when the Parkers' dance was put off, and then old Mr. Parker died; and nearly the same thing happened with the Normantons, only it was an uncle in that case?'

'Moral—never put off a dance, in case somebody dies.'

'Oh, hush, please!' groaned Nan, in a shocked voice; 'I don't like to hear you talk about such dreadful things. After all, it is such delicious weather that I am not sure a garden-party will not be more enjoyable; and you know, Dulce, that we are to dance on the lawn if we like.'

'And supposing it should rain,' put in that extremely troublesome young person, at which suggestion Dick looked very gloomy.

'In that case I think we must persuade

Mrs. Mayne to clear a room for us,' returned Nan cheerfully. 'If your mother consults me,' she continued, addressing Dick, who visibly brightened at this, 'I shall recommend her to empty the front drawing-room as much as possible. There is the grand piano, or the band might come indoors; there will be plenty of room for the young people, and the non-dancers can be drafted off into the inner drawing-room and conservatory.'

'What a head you have!' exclaimed Dick admiringly; and Phillis, who had not joined in the argument, was pleased to observe that she was quite of Nan's opinion—dancing was imperative, and if the lawns were wet they must manage indoors somehow. 'It would never do for people to be bored and listless,' finished the young lady sententiously, and such was Phillis's cleverness that it was understood at once that the oracle had spoken; but then it was never known for Nan and Phillis to differ.

Things being thus amicably arranged, the rest of the conversation flowed evenly on every other point, such as the arrangements of the tennis-matches in the large meadow, and the exact position of the marquees; but just as they were leaving the table Dick said another word to Nan in a somewhat low voice:

'It is all very well, but this sort of thing does make a fellow feel such a conceited fool.'

'If I were you I would not think about it at all,' she returned, in her sensible way. 'The neighbourhood will expect something of the kind, and we owe a little to other people; then it pleases your mother to make a fuss, as you call it, and it would be too ungrateful to disappoint her.'

'Well, perhaps you are right,' he returned in a slightly mollified tone, for he was a modest young fellow, and the whole business had occasioned him some soreness of spirit. 'Take it all in all, one has an awful lot to go through in life: there are the measles, you know, and whooping-cough, and the dentist, and one's examination, and no end of unpleasant things—but to be made by one's own mother to feel like an idiot for a whole afternoon! Never mind, it can be got through somehow,' finished the young philosopher, with a sigh that sent Nan into a fit of laughter.

## CHAPTER II.

#### DICK OBJECTS TO THE MOUNTAINS.

'SHALL we have our usual stroll?' asked Phillis, as Nan and Dick joined her at the window.

This was one of the customs at Glen Cottage. When any such fitting escort offered itself, the three girls would put on their hats, and, regardless of the evening dews and their crisp white dresses, would saunter, under Dick's guidance, through the quiet village, or down and up the country roads, 'just for a breath of air,' as they would say.

It is only fair to Mrs. Challoner's views of propriety to say, that she would have trusted her three pretty daughters to no other young man but Dick; and of late certain prudential doubts had crossed her mind. It was all very well for Phillis to say Dick was Dick, and there was an end of it. After all he belonged to the phalanx of her enemies, those shadowy invaders of her hearth that threatened her maternal peace. Dick was not a boy any longer; he had outgrown his hobbledehoy ways; the slight sandy moustache that he so proudly caressed was not a greater proof of his manhood than the undefinable change that had passed over his manners.

Mrs. Challoner began to distrust these evening strolls, and to turn over in her own mind various wary pretexts for detaining Nan on the next occasion.

'Just this once, perhaps, it does not matter,' she murmured to herself, as she composed herself to her usual nap.

'We shall not be long, little mother, so you must not be dull,' Dulce had said, kissing her lightly over her eyes. This was just one of the pleasant fictions at the cottage —one of those graceful little deceptions that are so harmless in families.

Dulce knew of those placid after-dinner

naps. She knew her mother's eyes would only unclose when Dorothy brought in the tea-tray; but she was also conscious that nothing would displease her mother more than to notice this habit. When they lingered indoors, and talked in whispers so as not to disturb her, Mrs. Challoner had an extraordinary facility for striking into the conversation in a way that was somewhat confusing.

'I don't agree with you at all,' she would say, in a drowsy voice. 'Is it not time for Dorothy to bring in the tea? I wish you would all talk louder. I must be getting a little deaf, I think, for I don't hear half you say.'

'Oh, it was only nonsense talk, mammie,' Dulce would answer; and the sisterly chit-chat would recommence, and her mother's head nid-nodded on the cushions until the next interruption.

'We shall not have many more of these strolls,' observed Dick regretfully, as they all walked together through the village, and then branched off into a long country road, where the air blew freshly in their faces, and low mists hung over the meadow-land. Though it was not quite dark, there was a tiny moon, and the glimmer of a star or two; and there was a pleasant fragrance as of new-mown grass.

They were all walking abreast, and keeping step, and Dick was in the middle, with Nan beside him. Dulce was hanging on to her arm, and every now and then breaking into little snatches of song.

'How I envy you!' exclaimed Phillis. 'Think of spending three whole months in Switzerland! Oh, you lucky Dick!'

For the Maynes had decided to pass the long vacation in the Engadine. Some hints had been dropped that Nan should accompany them, but Mrs. Challoner had regarded the invitation with some disfavour, and Mrs. Mayne had not pressed the point. If only Nan had known! but her mother had in this matter kept her own counsel.

'I don't know about that,' dissented Dick; he was rather given to argue for the mere pleasure of opposition. 'Mountains and glaciers are all very well in their way; but I think, on the whole, I would as soon be here. You see I am so accustomed to mix with a lot of fellows, that I am afraid of finding the pater's sole company rather slow.'

'For shame!' remarked his usual monitress. But she spoke gently; in her heart she knew why Dick failed to find the mountains alluring.

'Why could not one of you girls join us?' he continued wrathfully. The rogue had fairly bullied the unwilling Mrs. Mayne into giving that invitation.

'Do ask her, mother; she will be such a nice companion for you when the pater and I are doing our climbing; do, there's a dear good soul!' he had coaxed. And the dear good soul, who was secretly jealous of Nan, and loved her about as much as mothers usually love an only son's choice, had bewailed her hard fate in secret, and had then stepped over to the cottage with a bland and cheerful exterior, which grew more cheerful as Mrs. Challoner's reluctance made itself felt.

'It is not wise; it will throw them so much together,' Nan's mother had said. 'If it were only Phillis or Dulce—but you must have noticed——'

'Oh yes, I have noticed!' returned Mrs. Mayne hastily. She was a stout, comely-looking woman, but beside Mrs. Challoner she looked like a housekeeper dressed in her mistress's smart clothes. Mrs. Mayne's dresses never seemed to belong to her; it could not be said that they fitted her ill, but there was a want of adaptability—a lack of taste that failed to accord with her florid style of beauty.

She had been a handsome woman when Richard Mayne married her, but a certain deepening of tints and broadening of contour had not improved the mistress of Longmead. Her husband was a decided contrast: he was a small, wiry man, with sharp features that expressed a great deal of shrewdness. Dick had got his sandy hair; but Richard Mayne, the elder, had not his son's honest, kindly eyes. Mr. Mayne's were small and twinkling; he had a way of looking at people between his half-closed lids, in a manner half-sharp and half-jocular.

He was not vulgar, far from it; but he had a homely air about him that spoke of the self-made man. He was rather fond of telling people that his father had been in trade in a small way, and that he himself had been the sole architect of his fortune. 'Look at Dick,' he would say: 'he would never have a penny, that fellow, unless I made it for him; he has come into the world to find his bread ready buttered. I had to be content with a crust as I could earn it. The lad's a cut above us both, though he has the good taste to try and hide it.'

This sagacious speech was very true. Dick would never have succeeded as a business man; he was too full of crotchets and speculations to be content to run in narrow grooves. The notion of money-making was abhorrent to him; the idea of a city life, with its hard rubs and drudgery, was utterly distasteful to him: 'One would have to mix with such a lot of cads,' he would say. 'English, pure and undefiled, is not always spoken. If I must work, I would rather have a turn at law or divinity; the three old women with the eye between them knows which.'

It could not be denied that Dick winced a little at his father's homely speeches; but in his heart he was both proud and fond of him, and was given to assert to a few of his closest friends 'that, take it all in all, and looking at other fellows' fathers, he was a rattling good sort, and no mistake.'

When Mrs. Challoner had entered her little protest against her daughter's acceptance of the invitation, Mrs. Mayne had risen and kissed her with some effusion as she took her leave.

'It is so nice of you to say this to me; of course I should have been pleased, delighted to have had Nan with us' (oh, Mrs. Mayne, fie for shame! when you want your boy to yourself)—' but all the same I think you are so wise.'

'Poor child, I am afraid I am refusing her a great treat,' returned Mrs. Challoner, in a tone of regret. It was the first time since her husband's death that she had ever decided anything without reference to her daughters; but for once her maternal fears were up in arms, and drove her to sudden resolution.

'Yes, but, as you observed, it would throw them so entirely together; and Dick is so young. Richard was only saying the other night, that he hoped the boy would not fancy himself in love for the next two years, as he did not approve of such early engagements.'

'Neither do I,' returned Mrs. Challoner quickly. 'Nothing would annoy me more than for one of my daughters to entangle herself with so young a man. We know the world too well for that, Mrs. Mayne. Why, Dick may fall in and out of love half-a-dozen times before he really makes up his mind.'

'Ah, that is what Richard says,' returned Dick's mother, with a sigh; in her heart she was not quite of her husband's opinion. She remembered how that long waiting wasted her own youth—waiting for what? For comforts that she would gladly have done without—for a well-furnished house, when she would have lived happily in the poorest lodging with the Richard Mayne who had won her heart—for whom she would have toiled and slaved with the self-abnegating devotion of a loving woman; only he feared to have it so.

'"When poverty enters the door, love flies out of the window;" we had better make up our minds to wait, Bessie. I can work better in single than double harness just now.' That was what he said to her; and Bessie waited—not till she grew thin, but stout, and the spirit of her youth was gone; and it was a sober, middle-aged woman who took possession of the long-expected home.

Mrs. Mayne loved her husband, but during that tedious engagement her ardour had a little cooled, and it may be doubted whether the younger Richard was not dearer to her than his father; which was ungrateful, to say the least of it, as Mr. Mayne doated on his comely wife, and thought Bessie as handsome now as in the days when she came out smiling to welcome him—a slim young creature, with youthful roses in her cheeks.

From this brief conversation it may be seen that none of the elders quite approved of this budding affection. Mrs. Challoner, who belonged to a good old family, found it hard to forgive the Maynes' lowliness of birth; and, though she liked Dick, she thought Nan could do better for herself. Mr. Mayne poohpoohed the whole thing so entirely, that the women could only speak of it among themselves.

'Dick is a clever fellow; he ought to marry money,' he would say. 'I am not a millionaire, and a little more would be acceptable;' and though he was always kind to Nan and her sisters, he was for ever dealing sly hits at her. 'Phillis has the brains of the family,' he would say; 'that is the girl for my money. I call her a vast deal better-looking than Nan, though people make such a fuss about the other one;' a speech he was never tired of repeating in his son's presence, and at which Dick snapped his finger metaphorically, and said nothing.

When Dick wished that one of them were going to Switzerland, Nan sighed furtively. Dick was going away for three months, for the remainder of the long vacation. After next week they would not see him until Christmas—nearly six months. A sense of dreariness, as new as it was strange, swept momentarily over Nan as she pondered this. The summer months would be grievously clouded. Dick had been the moving spirit of all the fun: the tennis-parties, the pleasant dawdling afternoons, would lose their zest when he was away.

She remembered how persistently he had haunted their footsteps. When they paid visits to the Manor House, or Gardenhurst, or Fitzroy Lodge, Dick was sure to put in an appearance. People had nicknamed him the 'Challoners' Squire;' but now Nan must go squireless for the rest of the summer, unless she took compassion on Stanley Parker, or that dreadful chatterbox, his cousin.

The male population was somewhat sparse at Oldfield. There were a few Eton boys, and one or two in that delightful transition age when youth is most bashful and uninteresting —a sort of unfledged manhood, when the smooth boyish cheek contradicts the deepened bass of the voice—an age that has not ceased to blush, and which is full of aggravating idiosyncrasies and unexpected angles.

To be sure, Lord Fitzroy was a splendid specimen of a young guardsman, but he had lately taken to himself a wife; and Sir Alfred Mostyn, who was also somewhat attractive and a very pleasant fellow, and unattached at present, had a tiresome habit of rushing off to Norway, or St. Petersburg, or Niagara, or the Rocky Mountains, for what he termed sport, or a lark.

'It seems we are very stupid this evening,'

observed Phillis, for Dick had waxed almost as silent as Nan. 'I think the mother must nearly have finished her nap, so I propose we go back and have some tea;' and as Nan languidly acquiesced, they turned their faces towards the village again, Dulce still holding firmly to Nan's arm. By-and-by Dick struck out in a fresh direction.

'I say, don't you wish we could have last week over again?'

'Yes, oh yes! was it not too delicious!' from the three girls; and Nan added, 'I never enjoyed anything so much in my life,' in a tone so fervent that Dick was delighted.

'What a brick your mother was, to be sure, to spare you all!'

'Yes; and she was so dull, poor dear, all the time we were away. Dorothy gave us quite a pitiful account when we got home.'

'It was a treat one ought to remember all one's life,' observed Phillis, quite solemnly; and then ensued a most animated discussion.

The treat to which Phillis alluded had been simply perfect in the three girls' eyes. Dick, who never forgot his friends, had so worked upon his mother that she had consented to chaperon the three sisters during Commemoration; and a consent being fairly coaxed out of Mrs. Challoner, the plan was put into execution.

Dick, who was in the seventh heaven of delight, found roomy lodgings in the High Street, in which he installed his enraptured guests.

The five days that followed were simply hours snatched out of fairyland to these four happy young creatures; no wonder envious looks were cast at Dick as he walked in Christ Church Meadows with Nan and Dulce, Phillis bringing up the rear somewhat soberly with Mrs. Mayne.

'One pretty face would content most fellows,' his friends grumbled; 'but when you come to three, and not his own sisters either, why, it isn't fair on other folk.' And to Dick they said, 'Come, it is no use being so awfully close. Of course we see what's up; you are a lucky dog. Which is it, Mayne—the pretty one with the pink and white complexion, or the quiet one in grey, or the one with the mischievous eyes?'

'Faix, they are all darlints and jewels,

bless their purty faces!' drawled one young rogue, in his favourite brogue. 'Here's the top of the morning to ye, Mayne; and it is Mavourneen with the brown eyes and the trick of the smile like the sunshine's glint that has stolen poor Paddy's heart.'

'Oh, shut up, you fellows!' returned Dick, in a disgusted voice. 'What is the good of your pretending to be Irish, Hamilton, when you are a canny Scotchman?'

'Hoots, man, mind your clavers! You need not grizzle at a creature because he admires a wee gairl that is just beyond the lave—a sonsie wee thing with a glint in her e'en like diamonds.'

'Hamilton, will you leave off this foolery?'

'Nae doubt, nae doubt; would his honour pe axing if he pe wrang in the head, puir thing? Never mind that, put pe giving me the skene-dhu, or I will fight with proadswards like a gentleman for the bit lassie;' but here a wary movement on Dick's part extinguished the torrent of Highland eloquence, and brought the canny Scotchman to the ground.

Perfectly oblivious of all these compliments,

the Challenors enjoyed themselves with the zest of healthy, happy English girls. They were simply indefatigable; poor Mrs. Maynard succumbed utterly before the five days were over.

They saw the procession of boats; they were at the flower-show at Worcester; Sunday afternoon found them in the Broad Walk; and the next night they were dancing at the University ball.

They raved about the beauty of Magdalen cloisters; they looked down admiringly into the deer-park; Addison's Walk became known to them, and the gardens of St. John's. Phillis talked learnedly about Cardinal Wolsey as she stood in Christ Church hall; and in the theatre 'the young ladies in pink' invoked the most continuous cheers.

'Can they mean us?' whispered Dulce, rather alarmed, to their faithful escort Dick. 'I don't see any other pink dresses!'

And Dick said calmly:

'Well, I suppose so. Some of those fellows up there are such a trumpery lot.'

So Dulce grew more reassured.

But the greatest fun of all was the afternoon spent in Dick's room, when all his special friends were bidden to five o'clock tea, over which Nan, in her white gown, presided so gracefully.

What a dear, shabby old room it was, with old-fashioned window-seats, where one could look down into the quadrangle! Dick was an Oriel man, and thought his college superior even to Magdalen.

It became almost too hot and crowded at last, so many were the invitations given; but then, as Dick said afterwards, 'he was such a soft-hearted beggar, that he could not refuse the fellows that pestered him for invitations.'

Mrs. Mayne, looking very proud and happy, sat fanning herself in one of these windows. Phillis and Dulce were in the other, attended by that rogue Hamilton, and half a dozen more. Nan was the centre of another clique, who hemmed her and the tea-table in so closely, that Dick had to wander disconsolately round the outskirts; there was no getting a look from Nan that afternoon.

How hot it was! It was a grand *coup* when the door opened, and the scout made his appearance carrying a tray of ices.

'It is well to be Mayne!' half grumbled young Hamilton, as Dulce took one gratefully from his hand. 'He is treating us like a prince, instead of the thin-bread-and-butter entertainment he led us to expect. Put down that tea, Miss Challoner; I see iced claret-cup and strawberries in the corner. There is nothing like being an only child—doating parents are extremely useful articles. I am one of ten; would you believe it?' continued the garrulous youth. 'When one has six brothers older than one's self, I will leave you to imagine the consequences.'

'How nice!' returned Dulce innocently; 'I have always so longed for a brother. If it had not been for Dick, we should have had no one to do things for us.'

'Oh, indeed! Mayne is a sort of adopted brother!' observed her companion, looking at her rather sharply.

'We have always looked upon him as one. We do just as we like with him—scold and tease him, and send him on our errands;' which intelligence fairly convinced the envious Hamilton that the youngest Miss Challoner was not his friend's fancy.

Dick always recalled that evening with a sense of pride. How well and gracefully Nan had fulfilled her duties! how pretty she had looked, in spite of her flushed cheeks! He had never seen a girl to compare with her— not he!

They were so full of these delightful reminiscences, that they were at the cottage gate before they knew it; and then Dick astonished them by refusing to come in. He had quite forgotten, he said; but his mother had asked him to come home early, as she was not feeling just the thing.

'Quite right; you must do as she wishes,' returned Nan, dismissing him far too readily, as he thought; but she said 'Good-night!' with so kind a smile after that, that the foolish young fellow felt his pulses quicken.

Dick lingered at the corner until the cottage door was closed, and then he raced down the Longmead shrubbery, and set the house-bell pealing.

'They are in the library, I suppose?' he asked of the butler who admitted him; and, on receiving an answer in the affirmative, he dashed unceremoniously into the room, while his mother held up her finger, and smiled at the truant.

'You naughty boy, to be so late; and now you have spoiled your father's nap!' she said, pretending to scold him.

'Tut! tut! what nonsense you talk sometimes!' said Mr. Mayne rather crossly, as he stood on the hearthrug rubbing his eyes. 'I was not asleep, I will take my oath of that; only I wish Dick could sometimes enter a room without making people jump;' by which Dick knew that his father was in one of his contrary moods, when he could be very cross—very cross indeed!

## CHAPTER III.

MR. MAYNE MAKES HIMSELF DISAGREEABLE.

THE library at Longmead was a very pleasant room, and it was the custom of the family to retire thither on such occasions when guests were not forthcoming; and Mr. Mayne could indulge in his favourite nap without fear of interruption.

A certain simplicity, not to say homeliness, of manners prevailed in the house. It was understood among them that the dining-room was far too gorgeous for anything but occasions of ceremony. Mrs. Mayne, indeed, had had the good taste to cover the satin couches with pretty, fresh-looking cretonne, and had

had arranged hanging cupboards of old china until it had been transformed into a charming apartment, notwithstanding which the library was declared to be the family-room, where the usual masculine assortment of litter could be regarded with indulgent eyes, and where papers and pamphlets lay in delightful confusion.

Longmead was not a pretentious house; it was a moderately sized residence, adapted to a gentleman of moderate means: but in summer no place could be more charming. The broad gravel walk before the house had a background of roses; hundreds of roses climbed up the railings or twined themselves about the steps; a tiny miniature lake, garnished with water-lilies, lay in the centre of the lawn; a group of old elm-trees were beside it; behind the house lay another lawn, and beyond were meadows where a few sheep were quietly grazing. Mr. Mayne, who found time hang a little heavily on his hands, prided himself a good deal on his poultry-yard and kitchen-garden. A great deal of his spare time was spent among his favourite Bantams and Dorkings, and in superintending his opinionated old gardener: on summer mornings he would be out among the dews in his old coat and planter's hat, weeding among the gooseberry-bushes.

'It is the early bird that finds the worm,' he would say, when Dick sauntered into the breakfast-room later on; for in common with the youth of this generation he had a wholesome horror of early rising, which he averred was one of the barbarous usages of the dark ages in which his elders had been bred.

'I never took any interest in worms, sir,' returned Dick, helping himself to a tempting rasher that had just been brought in hot for the pampered youth. 'By-the-bye, have you seen Darwin's work on "The Formation of Vegetable Mould"? he declares "worms have played a more important part in the history of the world than most people would at first suppose;" they were our earliest ploughmen.'

'Oh, ah! indeed, very interesting!' observed his father drily; 'but all the same, I beg to observe, no one succeeded in life who was not an early riser.'

'A sweeping assertion, and one I might be

tempted to argue, if it were not for taking up your valuable time,' retorted Dick lazily, but with a twinkle in his eye. 'I know my constitution better than to trust myself out before the world is properly aired and dried. I am thinking it is less a case of worms than of rheumatism some early birds will be catching;' to which Mr. Mayne merely returned an ungracious 'Pshaw!' and marched off, leaving his son to enjoy his breakfast in peace.

When Dick entered the library on the evening in question, Mr. Mayne's querulous observation as to the noisiness of his entrance convinced him at once that his father was in a very bad humour indeed, and that on this account it behoved him to be exceedingly cool.

So he kissed his mother, who looked at him a little anxiously, and then sat down and turned out her work-basket as he had done Nan's two or three hours ago.

'You are late after all, Dick,' she said, with a little reproach in her voice. It was hardly a safe observation, to judge by her husband's cloudy countenance; but the poor thing sometimes felt her evenings a trifle dull when Dick was away. Mr. Mayne would take up his paper, but his eyes soon closed over it; that habit of seeking for the early worm rather disposed him to somnolent evenings, during which his wife knitted and felt herself nodding off out of sheer *ennui* and dulness. These were not the hours she had planned during those years of waiting; she had told herself that Richard would read to her or talk to her as she sat over her work, that they would have so much to say to each other; but now as she regarded his sleeping countenance evening after evening, it may be doubted whether matrimony was quite what she expected, since its bliss was so temperate and so strongly infused with drowsiness.

Dick looked up innocently. 'Am I late, mother?'

'Oh, of course not,' returned his father, with a sneer: 'it is not quite time to ring for Nicholson to bring our candles. Bessie, I think I should like some hot water to-night; I feel a little chilly;' and Bessie rang the bell obediently, and without any surprise in her manner. Mr. Mayne often woke up chilly from his long nap.

'Are you going to have a "drap of the

cratur"?' asked his son, with alacrity; 'well, I don't mind joining you, and that's the truth, for we have been dawdling about, and I am a trifle chilly myself.'

'You know I object to spirits for young men,' returned Mr. Mayne severely; 'nevertheless he pushed the whisky to Dick as soon as he had mixed his own glass, and his son followed his example.

'I am quite of your opinion, father,' he observed, as he regarded the handsome cut-glass decanter somewhat critically; 'but there are exceptions to every rule, and when one is chilly——'

'I wish you would make an exception and stay away from the cottage sometimes,' returned Mr. Mayne, with ill-suppressed impatience; 'it was all very well when you were all young things together, but it is high time matters should be different.'

Dick executed a low whistle of surprise and dismay. He had no idea his father's irritability had arisen from any definite cause. What a fool he had been to be so late! it might lead to some unpleasant discussion. Well, after all, if his father chose to be so disagreeable it was not his fault; and he was no longer a boy to be chidden, or made to do this or that against his own will.

Mr. Mayne was sufficiently shrewd to see that his son was somewhat taken aback by this sudden onslaught, and he was not slow to press his advantage. He had wanted to give Dick a bit of his mind for some time, and after all there is no time like the present.

'Yes, it was all very well when you were a lot of children together,' he continued, in his most dictatorial manner. 'Of course, it is hard on you, Dick, having no brothers and sisters to keep you company; your mother and I were always sorry about that for your sake.'

'Oh, don't mention it,' interrupted Dick; 'on the whole, I am best pleased as it is.'

'But it would have been better for you,' returned his father sharply; 'we should not have had all this fooling and humbug if you had had sisters of your own.'

'Fooling and humbug!' repeated Dick hotly; 'I confess, sir, I don't quite understand to what you are referring.' He was growing very angry, but his mother flung herself between the combatants.

'Don't, my boy, don't; you must not answer your father in that way. Richard, what makes you so hard on him to-night? It must be the gout, Dick; we had better send for Dr. Weatherby in the morning,' continued the anxious woman with tears in her eyes, 'for your dear father would never be so cross to you as this unless he were going to be ill.'

'Stuff and nonsense, Bessie! Dr. Weatherby indeed!' but his voice was less wrathful. 'What is it but fooling, I should like to know, for Dick to be daundering his time away with a parcel of girls as he does with these Challoners!'

'I suppose you were never a young man yourself, sir.'

'Oh yes, I was, my boy,' and the corners of Mr. Mayne's mouth relaxed in spite of his efforts to keep serious. 'I fell in love with your mother, and stuck to her for seven or eight years; but I did not make believe that I was brother to a lot of pretty girls, and waste all my time dancing attendance on them and running about on their errands.'

'You ought to have taken a lesson out of my book,' returned his son readily.

'No, I ought to have done no such thing, sir!' shouted back Mr. Mayne, waxing irate again. It could not be denied Dick could be excessively provoking when he liked. 'Don't I tell you it is time this sort of thing was stopped? Why, people will begin to talk, and say you are making up to one of them; it is not right, Dick—it is not indeed,' with an attempted pathos.

'I don't care that for what people say,' returned the young fellow, snapping his finger. 'Is it not a pity you are saying all this to me just when I am going away, and am not likely to see any of them for the next six months? You are very hard on me to-night, father; and I can't think what it is all about.'

Mr. Mayne was silent a moment, revolving his son's pathetic speech. It was true he had been cross, and had said more than he had meant to say. He had not wished to hinder Dick's innocent enjoyments; but if he were unknowingly picking flowers at the edge of a precipice, was it not his duty as a father to warn him?

'I think I have been a little hard, my lad,' he said candidly; 'but there, you and your mother know my bark is worse than my bite: I only wanted to warn you—that's all, Dick.'

'Warn me!—against what, sir?' asked the young man quickly.

'Against falling in love, really, with one of the Challoner girls!' returned Mr. Mayne, trying to evade the fire of Dick's eyes, and blustering a little in consequence. 'Why, they have not a penny, one of them; and if report be true, Mrs. Challoner's money is very shakily invested. Paine told me so the other day. He said he should never wonder if a sudden crash came any minute.'

'Is this true, Richard?'

'Paine declares it is; and think of Dick saddling himself with the support of a whole family!'

'It strikes me you are taking things very much for granted,' returned his son, trying to speak coolly, but flushing like a girl over his words. 'I think you might wait, father, until I proposed bringing you home a daughter-in-law.'

'I am only warning you, Dick, that the Challoner connection would be distasteful to me,' replied Mr. Mayne, feeling that he had gone a little too far. 'If you had brothers and sisters it would not matter half so much; but it would be too hard if my only son were to cross my wishes.'

'Should you disinherit me, father?' observed Dick cheerfully. He had recovered his coolness and pluck, and began to feel more equal to the occasion.

'We should see about that; but I hardly think it would be for your advantage to oppose me too much,' returned his father, with an ominous pucker of his eyebrows, which warned Dick that it was hardly safe to chaff the old boy too much to-night.

'I think I will go to bed, Richard,' put in poor Mrs. Mayne. She had wisely forborne to mix in the discussion, fearing that it would bring upon her the vials of her husband's wrath. Mr. Mayne was as choleric as a Welshman, and had a reserve force of sharp cynical sayings that were somewhat hard to bear. He was disposed to turn upon her on such occasions, and to accuse her of spoiling Dick and taking his part against his father; between the two Richards she sometimes had a very bad time indeed.

Dick lighted his mother's candle, and bade her good-night; but all the same she knew she had not seen the last of him. A few minutes afterwards there was a hasty tap at the bedroom door, and Dick thrust in his head.

'Come in, my dear; I have been expecting you,' she said, with a pleased smile. He always came to her when he was ruffled or put out, and brought her all his grievances; surely this was the very meaning and essence of her motherhood—this healing and comfort that lay in her power of sympathy.

When he was a little fellow, had she not extracted many a thorn and bound up many a cut finger? and now he was a man, would she be less helpful to him when he wanted a different kind of comfort?

'Come in, my son,' she said, beckoning him to the low chair beside her, into which Dick threw himself with a petulant yawn.

'Mother, what made the pater so hard on me to-night? he cut up as rough as though I had committed some crime.'

'I don't think he is quite himself to-night,' returned Mrs. Mayne, in her soft motherly voice. 'I fancy he misses you, Dick, and is half jealous of the Challoners for monopolizing you. You are all we have, that's where it is,' she finished, stroking the sandy head with her plump hand; but Dick jerked away from her with a little impatience.

'I think it rather hard that a fellow is to be bullied for doing nothing at all,' replied Dick, with a touch of sullenness. When the pater is in this humour it is no use saying anything to him; but you may as well tell him, mother, that I mean to choose my wife for myself.'

'Oh, my dear, I dare not tell him anything of the kind,' returned Mrs. Mayne, in an alarmed voice; and then, as she glanced at her son, her terror merged into amusement. There was something so absurdly boyish in Dick's appearance, such a ludicrous contrast between the manliness of his speech and his smooth cheek; the little fringe of hirsute ornament, of which Dick was so proud, was hardly visible in the dim light; his youthful figure, more clumsy than graceful, had an unfledged air about it: nevertheless, the boldness of his words took away her breath.

'Every man has a right to his own choice in such a matter,' continued Dick loftily. 'You may as well tell him, mother, that I intend to select my own wife.'

'My dear, I dare not for worlds——' she began; and then she stopped, and laid her hand on his shoulder. 'Why do you say this to me? there is plenty of time,' she went on hastily; 'that is what your father says, and I think he is right. You are too young for these sort of things yet. You must see the world—you must look about you—you must have plenty of choice,' continued the anxious mother. 'I shall be hard to please, Dick, for I shall think no one good enough for my boy; that is the worst of having only one, and he the best son that ever lived,' finished Mrs. Mayne, with maternal pride in her voice.

Dick took this effusion very coolly. He was quite used to all this sort of worship; he did not think badly of himself; he was not particularly humble-minded or given to troublesome introspection; on the whole, he thought himself a good fellow, and was not at all surprised that people appreciated him.

'There are such a lot of cads in the world, one is always glad to fall in with a different sort,' he would say to himself. He was quite of his mother's opinion, that an honest God-fearing young fellow, who spoke the truth and shamed the devil; who had no special vices but a dislike for early rising; who had tolerable brains, and more than his share of muscle; who was in the Oxford eleven, and who had earned his blue ribbon—that such an one might be considered to set an example to his generation.

When his mother told him she would be hard to please, Dick looked a little wicked and thought of Nan; but the name was not mentioned between them. Nevertheless, Mrs. Mayne felt with unerring maternal instinct that, in spite of his youth, Dick's choice was made, and sighed to herself at the thought of the evil days that were to come.

Poor woman, she was to have little peace that night! Hardly had Dick finished his grumble and sauntered away, before her husband's step was heard in his dressing-room.

'Bessie,' he called out to her, 'why do you allow that boy to keep you up so late at night? Do you know it is eleven, and you are still fully dressed?'

'Is it so late, Richard?'

'Yes, of course,' he snapped; 'but that is the care you take of your health; and the way you cosset and spoil that boy is dreadful.'

'I don't think Dick is easily spoiled,' plucking up a little spirit to answer him.

'That shows how little you understand boys,' returned her husband. Evidently the whisky, though it was the best Glenlivat, had failed to mollify him. It might be dangerous to go too far with Dick, for he had a way of turning round and defending himself that somewhat embarrassed Mr. Mayne, but with his wife there would be no such danger. He would dominate her by his sharp speeches, and reduce her to abject submission in a moment, for Bessie was the meekest of wives. 'Take care how you side with him,' he continued, in a threatening voice. 'He thinks that I am not serious in what I said just now, and is for carrying it off with a high hand; but I tell you, and you had better tell him, that I was never more in earnest in my life. I won't have one of those Challoner girls for a daughter-in-law!'

'Oh, Richard! and Nan is such a sweet girl!' returned his wife, with tears in her eyes. She was awfully jealous of Nan, at times she almost dreaded her; but for her boy's sake she would have taken her now to her heart, and defied even her formidable husband. 'She is such a pretty creature, too—no one can help loving her.'

'Pshaw!' returned her husband; 'pretty creature indeed! that is just your soft-hearted nonsense. Phillis is ten times prettier, and has heaps more sense. Why couldn't Dick have taken a fancy to her?'

'Because I am afraid he cares for the other one,' returned Mrs. Mayne sadly. She had no wish to deceive her husband, and she knew that the golden apple had rolled to Nan's feet.

'Stuff and rubbish!' he responded wrathfully. 'What is a boy of his age to know about such things? Tell him from me to put this nonsense out of his head for the next year or two; there is plenty of time to look out for a wife after that. But I won't have him making up his mind until he has left Oxford.' And Mrs. Mayne, knowing that her husband had spoken his last word, thankfully withdrew, feeling that in her heart she secretly agreed with him.

## CHAPTER IV.

### DICK'S FÊTE.

AS Mr. Mayne's wrath soon evaporated, and Dick was a sweet-tempered fellow, and bore no malice, this slight altercation produced no lasting effect, except that Dick, for the next few days, hurried home to his dinner, talked a good deal about Switzerland, and never mentioned a Challoner in his father's hearing.

'We must keep him in a good temper for the 25th,' he said to his mother, with a touch of the Mayne shrewdness.

That day was rapidly approaching, and all sorts of festive preparations were going on at Longmead. Dick himself gravely superintended the rolling of the tennis-ground in the large meadow; and daubed himself plentifully with lime in marking out the courts, while Mr. Mayne stood with his hands in the pockets of his shooting-coat watching him. The two were a great deal together just then. Dick rather stuck to his father during one or two mornings; the wily young fellow knew that Nan was closeted with his mother, helping her with all sorts of feminine arrangements, and he was determined to keep them apart. Nan wondered a great deal why Dick did not come to interrupt or tease them as usual, and grew a little absent over Mrs. Mayne's rambling explanations. When the gong sounded, no one asked her to stay to luncheon. Mrs. Mayne saw her put on her hat without uttering a single protest.

'It is so good of you to help me, dear,' she said, taking the girl into her embrace. 'You are quite sure people won't expect a sit-down supper?'

'Oh no; the buffet system is best,' returned Nan decidedly. 'Half the people will not stay, and you need not make a fuss about the rest. It is an afternoon party, you must remember that; only people who are very intimate will remain for the fun of the thing. Tell Nicholson to have plenty of ices going— people care most for that sort of refreshment.'

'Yes, dear; I will be sure to remember,' returned her friend meekly.

She was very grateful to Nan for these hints, and was quite willing to follow her guidance in all such matters; but when Nan proposed once sending for Dick to ask his opinion on some knotty point that baffled their women's wits, Mrs. Mayne demurred.

'It is a pity to disturb him, he is with his father; and we can settle these things by ourselves,' she replied, not venturing to mar the present tranquillity by sending such a message to Dick. Mr. Mayne would have accompanied his son, and the consultation would hardly have ended peaceably. 'Men have their hobbies. We had better settle all this together, you and I,' she said hurriedly.

Nan merely nodded, and cut the Gordian knot through somewhat ruthlessly; but on that occasion she put on her hat before the gong sounded.

'You must be very busy, for one never has

a glimpse of you in the morning,' she could not help saying to Dick, as he came in that afternoon to escort them to Fitzroy Lodge.

'Well, yes, I am tolerably busy,' he drawled. 'You see, I am never free to do things in the afternoons,' a fact that Nan felt was unanswerable.

When Nan and her sisters woke on the morning of the memorable day, the bright sunshine of a cloudless June day set all their fears at rest. If the sun smiled on Dick's fête, all would be well. If Nan's devotions were longer than usual that morning, no one was the wiser; if she added a little clause, calling down a blessing on a certain head, no one would be the poorer for such pure prayers; indeed, it were well if many such were uttered for the young men who go forth morning after morning into the temptations of life.

Such prayers might stretch like an invisible shield before the countless foes that environ such an one; fiery darts may be caught upon it; a deadly thrust may be turned away. What if the blessing would never reach the ear of the loved one, who goes out unconscious of sympathy. His guardian angel has heard it, and perchance it has reached the very gate of heaven.

Nan came down, smiling and radiant, to find Dick waiting for her in the veranda, and chattering to Phillis and Dulce.

'Why, Dick!' she cried, blushing with surprise and pleasure, 'to think of your being here on your birthday morning!'

'I only came to thank you and the girls for your lovely presents,' returned Dick, becoming rather incoherent and red at the sight of Nan's blush. 'It was so awfully good of you all, to work all those things for me;' for Nan had taken secret measurements in Dick's room, and had embroidered a most exquisite mantelpiece valance, and Phillis and Dulce had worked the corners of a green cloth with wonderful daffodils and bulrushes to cover Dick's shabby table; and Dick's soul had been filled with ravishment at the sight of these gifts.

Nan would not let him go on, but all the same his happy face delighted her.

'No, don't thank us; we liked doing it,' she returned rather coolly. 'You know we owed you something after all your splendid hospitality, and work is never any trouble to us.'

'But I never saw anything I liked better,' blurted out Dick; 'all the fellows will be jealous of me. I am sure I don't know what Hamilton will say. It was awfully good of you, Nan, and so it was of the others; and if I don't make it up to you somehow, my name is not Dick;' and he smiled round at them as he spoke. 'Fancy putting in all those stitches for me!' he thought to himself.

'We are so glad you are pleased,' returned Nan, with one of her sweet, straightforward looks; 'that is what we wanted to give you— a little surprise on your birthday. Now you must tell us about your other presents;' and Dick, nothing loath, launched into eloquent descriptions of the silver-fitted dressing-case from his mother, and the gun and thoroughbred collie that had been his father's gifts.

'He is such a fine fellow; I must show him to you this afternoon,' went on Dick eagerly. 'His name is Vigo, and he has such a superb head. Was it not good of the pater? he knew I had a fancy for a collie, and he has been in treaty for one ever so long. Is he not a dear old boy?' cried Dick rapturously. But he did not tell his friends of the crisp bundle of bank-notes with which Mr. Mayne had enriched his son; only, as Dick fingered them lovingly, he wondered what pretty foreign thing he could buy for Nan, and whether her mother would allow her to accept it.

After this Nan dismissed him somewhat peremptorily; he must go back to his breakfast, and allow them to do the same.

'Mind you come early,' were Dick's last words as he waved his straw hat to them. How often the memory of that morning recurred to him as he stood solitary and thoughtful, contemplating some grand stretch of Alpine scenery.

The snow-peaks and blue glaciers melted away before his eyes; in their place rose unbidden a picture framed in green trelliswork, over which roses were climbing.

Fresh girlish faces smiled back at him; the brightest and kindest of glances met his. 'Good-bye, Dick; a thousand good wishes from us all.' A slim white hand had gathered a

## Dick's Fête.

rosebud for him; how proudly he had worn it all that day! Stop, he had it still; it lay all crushed and withered in his pocket-book. He had written the date under it; one day he meant to show it to her. Oh foolish days of youth, so prodigal of minor memories and small deeds of gifts, when a withered flower can hold the rarest scent, and in a crumpled rose-leaf there is a whole volume of ecstatic meaning! Oh golden days of youth, never to be surpassed!

Never in the memory of Oldfield had there been a more delicious day.

The sky was cloudless; long purple shadows lay under the elm-trees; a concert of bird-music sounded from the shrubberies; in the green meadows flags were waving, tent draperies fluttering; the house-doors stood open, showing a flower-decked hall and vista of cool shadowy rooms.

Dick, looking bright and trim, wandered restlessly over the place, and Mr. Mayne fidgeted after him; while Mrs. Mayne sat fanning herself under the elm-trees, and hoping the band would not be late.

No—there it was turning in now at the

stable-entrance, and playing 'The Girl I left behind Me;' and there at the same moment was Nan coming up the lawn in her white gown, closely followed by her mother and sisters.

'Are we the first?' she asked, as Dick darted across the grass to meet her. 'That is nice; we shall see all the people arrive. How inspiriting that music is, and how beautiful everything looks!'

'It is awfully jolly of you to be the first,' whispered Dick; 'and how nice you look, Nan! You always do, you know; but to-day you are first-rate. Is this a new gown?' casting an approving look over Nan's costume, which was certainly very fresh and pretty.

'Oh yes; we have all new dresses in your honour, and we made them ourselves,' returned Nan carelessly. 'Mother has got her old silk, but for her it does not so much matter—at least that is what she says.'

'And she is quite right. She is always real splendid, as the Yankees say, whatever she wears,' returned Dick, wishing secretly that his mother, in her new satin dress, looked half so well as Mrs. Challoner in her old one.

But it was no use. Mrs. Mayne never set off her handsome dresses; with her flushed, good-natured face and homely ways, she showed to marked disadvantage beside Mrs. Challoner's faded beauty. Mrs. Challoner's gown might be antique, but nothing could surpass the quiet grace of her carriage, or the low pleasant modulations of her voice. Her figure was almost as slim as her daughters', and she could easily have passed for their elder sister.

Lady Fitzroy, who was a Burgoyne by birth—and everyone knows that for haughtiness and a certain exclusive intoleration none could match the Burgoynes—always distinguished Mrs. Challoner by the marked attention she paid her.

'A very ladylike woman, Percival. Certainly the most ladylike person in the neighbourhood,' she would say to her husband, who was not quite so exclusive, and always made himself pleasant to his neighbours; and she would ask very graciously after her brother-in-law, Sir Francis Challoner. 'He is still in India, I suppose?'

'Oh yes; he is still in India,' Mrs. Challoner would reply rather curtly. She had not the faintest interest in her husband's brother, whom she had never seen more than twice in her life, and who was understood to be small credit to his family. The aforesaid Sir Francis Challoner had been the poorest of English baronets. His property had dwindled down until it consisted simply of a half-ruined residence in the north of England.

In his young days Sir Francis had been a prodigal, and, like the prodigal in the parable, he had betaken himself into far countries, not to waste his substance, for he had none, but if possible to glean some of the Eastern riches.

Whether he had been successful or not Mrs. Challoner hardly knew. That he had married and settled in Calcutta—that he had a son named Harry who had once written to her in round hand, and subscribed himself as her affectionate nephew, Henry Ford Challoner— this she knew; but what manner of person Lady Challoner might be, or what sort of home her brother-in-law had made for himself, those points were enveloped in mystery.

'I suppose she is so civil to me because of your uncle Francis,' she used to say to her girls, which was attributing to Lady Fitzroy a degree of snobbishness that was quite undeserved. Lady Fitzroy really liked Mrs. Challoner, and found intercourse with her very pleasant and refreshing. When one is perfectly wellbred, there is a subtle charm in harmony of voice and manner. Mrs. Challoner might have dressed in rags if she liked, and the young Countess would still have aired her choicest smiles for her.

It was lucky Nan had those few words from Dick, for they fell apart after this, and were separated the greater portion of the afternoon.

Carriages began to drive in at the gates, groups of well-dressed people thronged the lawn, and were draughted off to the field where the band was playing.

Nan and her sisters had their work cut out for them; they knew everybody, and they were free of the house. It was they who helped Dick arrange the tennis-matches; who pointed out to the young men of the party which was the tea-tent, and where the ices and claret-cup were to be found. They marshalled the older ladies into pleasant nooks, where they could be sheltered from the sun, and see all that was going on.

'No, thank you; I shall not play tennis this afternoon; there are too many of us, and I am so busy,' Nan said, dismissing one after another who came up to her. 'If you want a partner, there is Carrie Paine, who is dying for a game.'

Dick, who was passing with Lady Fitzroy on his arm, whom he was hurrying somewhat unceremoniously across the field, threw her a grateful glance as he went by.

'What a sweet-looking girl that is!' said Lady Fitzroy graciously, as she panted a little over her exertion.

'Who—Nan? Yes; isn't she a brick— and the others too?' for Phillis and Dulce were just as self-denying in their labours. As Mr. Mayne said afterwards, 'They were just everywhere, those Challoners, like a hive of swarming bees;' which, as it was said in a grumbling tone, was ungrateful, to say the least of it.

Dick worked like a horse too; he looked all the afternoon as though he had a tough job in hand that required the utmost gravity

# Dick's Fête.

and despatch. He was for ever hurrying elderly ladies across the field towards the refreshment-tent, where he deposited them, panting and heated, in all sorts of corners.

'Are you quite comfortable? May I leave you now; or shall I wait and take you back again?' asked Dick, who was eager for a fresh convoy.

'No, no; I would rather stay here a little,' returned Mrs. Paine, and who was not desirous of another promenade with the hero of the day. 'Go and fetch some one else, Dick; I am very well off where I am,' exchanging an amused glance with one of her friends, as Dick, hot and breathless, started off on another voyage of discovery.

Dick's behaviour had been simply perfect all the afternoon in his father's eyes; but later on, when the band struck up a set of quadrilles, he committed his first solecism in manners—instead of asking Lady Fitzroy to dance with him, he hurried after Nan.

'This is our dance—come along,' he said, taking her unwilling hand; but she held back a moment.

'Are you sure? Is there not some one

else you ought to choose—Lady Fitzroy, for example?' questioned Nan, with admirable forethought.

'Bother Lady Fitzroy!' exclaimed Dick, under his breath; he had had quite enough of that lady. 'Why are you holding back, Nan, in this fashion?' a cloud coming over his face. 'Haven't you promised weeks ago to give me the first dance?' And Nan, seeing the cloud on his face, yielded without another word. Dick always managed to have his own way somehow.

'Dick! Dick!' cried his father in a voice of agony, as they passed him.

'All in good time—coming presently,' returned the scapegrace cheerfully. 'Now, Nan, this is our place. We will have Hamilton and Dulce for our *vis-à-vis*. What a jolly day! and isn't this first-rate!' exclaimed Dick, rubbing his hands, and feeling as though he were only just beginning to enjoy himself.

Nan was not quite so easy in her mind.

'Your father does not look very pleased. I am afraid, after all, you ought to have asked Lady Fitzroy,' she said, in a low voice; but Dick turned a deaf ear. He showed her the rose in his button-hole; and when Nan told him it was withered, and wanted him to take it out, he gave her a reproachful look that made her blush.

They were very happy after this; and, when the dance was over, Dick gave her his arm, and carried her off to see Vigo, who was howling a deep mournful bass at the back of the gardener's cottage.

Nan made friends with him, and stroked his black curly head, and looked lovingly into his deep melancholy eyes; and then, as her flowers were fading, they strolled off into the conservatory, where Dick gathered her a fresh bouquet, and then sat down and watched her arrange it.

'What clever fingers you have got!' he said, looking at them admiringly, as Nan sorted the flowers in her lap; and at this unlucky moment they were discovered by Mr. Mayne, who was bringing Lady Fitzroy to see a favourite orchid.

He shot an angry suspicious glance at his son.

'Dick, your mother is asking for you,' he

said, rather abruptly; but Dick growled something in an undertone, and did not move.

Nan gave him a frightened nudge. Why was he so imprudent?

'I cannot move, because of my flowers; do go, Dick. You must indeed, if your mother wants you;' and she looked at him in such a pleading way, that Dick dared not refuse. It was just like his father to come and disturb his first happy moments, and to order him off to go and do something disagreeable. He had almost a mind to brave it out, and remain, in spite of him; but there was Nan looking at him in a frightened, imploring way.

'Oh, do go, Dick,' giving him a little impatient push in her agitation—' if your mother wants you; you must not keep her waiting.' But Nan in her heart knew, as Dick did in his, that the message was only a subterfuge to separate them.

## CHAPTER V.

'I AM QUITE SURE OF HIM.'

NAN would willingly have effected her escape too, but she was detained by the flowers that Dick had tossed so lightly into her lap. She was rather dismayed at her position, and her fingers trembled a little over their work. There was a breath—a sudden entering current of antagonism and prejudice that daunted her. Lady Fitzroy cast an admiring look at the girl, as she sat there with glowing cheeks and downcast lids.

'How pretty she is!' she said in a low voice, as Mr. Mayne pointed out his favourite orchid. 'She is like her mother; there is just the same quiet style, only I suspect Mrs.

Challoner was even better-looking in her time.'

'Humph! yes, I suppose so,' returned her host, in a dissatisfied tone. He had not brought Lady Fitzroy there to talk of the Challoners, but to admire his orchids. Then he shot another glance at Nan between his half-closed eyes, and a little spice of malice flavoured his next words.

'Shall we sit here a moment? Let me see—you were asking me, Lady Fitzroy, about Dick's prospects. I was talking to his mother about them the other day. I said to her then, Dick must settle in life well—he must marry money.'

'Indeed,' replied Lady Fitzroy, somewhat absently; she even indulged in a slight yawn behind her fan. She liked Dick well enough, as everyone else did, but she was not partial to his father. How tiresome it was of Fitzroy to insist so much on their neighbourly duties.

Mr. Mayne was not 'one of them,' as she would have phrased it; he did not speak their language, or lead their life; their manners and customs, their little tricks and turns of thought, were hieroglyphics to him.

A man who had never had a grandfather—at least a grandfather worth knowing; whose father's hands had dabbled in trade—actually trade—such an one might be a very worthy man, an excellent citizen, an exemplary husband and father, but it behoved a woman in her position not to descend too freely to his level.

'Percival is such a sad Radical,' she would say to herself; 'he does not make sufficient distinction between people: I should wish to be neighbourly, but I cannot bring myself to be familiar with these Maynes;' which was perhaps the reason why Lady Fitzroy was not as popular at Longmead and in other places as her good-natured husband.

'Oh, indeed,' she said, with difficulty repressing another slight yawn behind her fan, but speaking in a fatigued voice; but Mr. Mayne was too intent on his purpose to notice it.

'If Dick had brothers and sisters it would not matter so much; but when one has only a single hope—eh, Lady Fitzroy!—things must be a little different then.'

'He will have plenty of choice,' she returned, with an effort at graciousness. 'Oldfield is rich in pretty girls——' and she cast another approving glance at poor Nan, but Mr. Mayne interrupted her almost rudely.

'Ah, as to that,' he returned with a sneer, 'we want no such nonsense for Dick. Here are the facts of the case. Here is an honest, good-tempered young fellow, but with no particular push in him; he has money, you say—yes, but not enough to give him the standing I want him to have. I am ambitious for Dick. I want him to settle in life well. Why, he might be called to the Bar—he might enter Parliament; there is no limit to a man's career nowadays. I will do what I can for him, but he must meet me half-way.'

'You mean,' observed Lady Fitzroy, with a little perplexity in her tone, 'that he must look out for an heiress.' She was not in the secret, and she could not understand why her host was treating her to this outburst of confidence. 'It was so disagreeable to be mixed up with these sort of things,' as she told her husband afterwards. 'I never knew him quite so odious before; and there was that pretty Miss Challoner sitting near us, and he never let me address a word to her.

Nan began to feel she had had enough of it. She started up hastily as Lady Fitzroy said the last words, but the entrance of some more young people compelled her to stand inside a moment, and she heard Mr. Mayne's answer distinctly. 'Well, not an heiress exactly; but the girl I have in view for him has a pretty little sum of money, and the connection is all that could be wished; she is nice-looking too, and is a bright, taking little body——' But here Nan made such a resolute effort to pass, that the rest of the sentence was lost upon her.

Dick, who was strolling up and down the lawn rather discontentedly, hurried up to her as she came out.

'They are playing a valse; come, Nan,' he said, holding out his hand to her with his usual eagerness; but she shook her head.

'I cannot dance, I am too tired; there are others you ought to ask.' She spoke a little ungraciously, and Dick's face wore a look of dismay, as she walked away from him with quick even footsteps.

Tired? Nan tired! he had never heard of such a thing. What had put her out? The sweet brightness had died out of her eyes, and her cheeks were flaming. Should he follow her and have it out with her, there and then? But as he hesitated, young Hamilton came over the grass and linked his arm in his.

'Come and introduce me to that girl in blue gauze, or whatever you call that flimsy manufacture. Come along, there's a good fellow,' he said coaxingly—and Dick's opportunity was lost.

But he was wrong; for once in her life Nan was tired; the poor girl felt a sudden quenching of her bright elasticity that amounted to absolute fatigue.

She had spoken to Dick sharply; but that was to get rid of him, and to recall him to a sense of his duty. Not for worlds would she be seen dancing with him or even talking to him again!

She sat down on a stump of a tree in the shrubbery, and wondered wearily what had taken it out of her so much. And then she recalled sentence by sentence everything that had passed in the conservatory.

She had found out quite lately that Mr.

Mayne did not approve of her intimacy with Dick. His manner had somewhat changed to her, and several times he had spoken to her in a carping, fault-finding way—little cut-and-dried sentences of elderly wisdom that she had not understood at the time.

She had not pleased him of late somehow, and all her little efforts and overtures had been lost upon him. Nan had been quite aware of this, but it had not troubled her much; it was a way he had, and he meant nothing by it. Most men had humours that must be respected, and Dick's father had his. So she bore herself very sweetly towards him, treating his caustic remarks as jokes, and laughing pleasantly at them, never taking his hints in earnest—he would know better some day, that was all; but she had no idea of any deeply laid plan against their happiness. She felt as though some one had struck her hard; she had received a blow that set all her nerves tingling. It was very funny what he said; it was so droll that it almost made her laugh, and yet her eyes smarted, and her cheeks felt on fire.

'"Dick must marry money." Why must

he?—that was so droll. "Well, not an heiress exactly, but a pretty little sum of money, and a bright, taking little body." Who was this mysterious person whom he had in view, whose connections were so desirable, who was to be Dick's future wife? Dick's future wife!' repeated Nan, with an odd little quiver of her lip. 'And was it not droll, settling it all for him like that?'

Nan fell into a brown study, and then woke up with a little gasp. It was all clear to her now; all those little cut-and-dried sentences —all those veiled sneers and innuendoes.

They were poor—poor as church-mice— and Dick must marry money. Mr. Mayne had laid his plans for his son, and was watching their growing intimacy with disapproving eyes. Perhaps 'the bright, taking little body' might accompany them to Switzerland; perhaps among the mountains Dick would forget her, and lend a ready acquiescence to his father's plans. Who was she? Had Nan ever seen her? Could she be here this afternoon—this future rival and enemy of her peace?

'Ah, what nonsense I am thinking!' she

exclaimed to herself, starting up with a little shame and impatience at her own thoughts. 'What has this all got to do with me? let them settle it between them—money-bags and all. Dick is Dick, and after all I am not afraid!' and Nan marched back to the company, with her head higher, and a great assumption of cheerfulness, and a little gnawing feeling of discomfort at her heart, to which she would not have owned for worlds.

Nan was the gayest of the gay that evening, but she would not dance again with Dick; she sent the poor boy away from her with a decision and peremptoriness that struck him with fresh dismay.

'You are not tired now, Nan; you have been waltzing ever so long with Cathcart and Hamilton.'

'Never mind about me to-night; you must go and ask Lady Fitzroy. No, I am not cross. Do you think I would be cross to you on your birthday? but all the same I will not have you neglect your duties. Go and ask her this moment, sir!' and Nan smiled in his face in the most bewitching way, and gave a little flutter to her fan. She accepted Mr.

Hamilton's invitation to a valse under Dick's very eyes, and whirled away on his arm, while Dick stood looking at her ruefully.

Just at the very last moment Nan's heart relented.

'Walk down to the gate with us,' she whispered, as she passed him on her way to the cloak-room.

Dick, who was by this time in a somewhat surly humour, made no sort of response; nevertheless Nan found him out on the gravel path waiting for them, in company with Cathcart and Hamilton.

Nan shook off the latter rather cleverly, and took Dick's arm, in cheerful unconsciousness of his ill-humour.

'It is so good of you to come with us. I wanted to get you a moment to myself, to congratulate you on the success of the evening. It was admirably managed, everyone says so; even Lady Fitzroy was pleased, and her ladyship is a trifle fastidious. Have the band indoors, and set them to dancing—that is what I said; and it has turned out a complete success,' finished Nan, with a little gush of enthusiasm; but she did not find Dick responsive.

'Oh! bother the success and all that!' returned that very misguided young man; 'it was the slowest affair to me, I assure you, and I am thankful it is over. You have spoiled the evening to me, and that is what you have done,' grumbled Dick, in his most ominous voice.

'I spoilt your evening, you ungrateful boy!' replied Nan innocently; but she smiled to herself in the darkness, and the reproach was sweet to her. They had entered the garden of Glen Cottage by this time, and Dick was fiercely marching her down a side-path that led to the kitchen. The hall-door stood open. Cathcart and Hamilton were chattering with the girls in the porch, while Mrs. Challoner went inside. They peered curiously into the summer dusk, as Dick's impatient footsteps grated on the gravel path.

'I spoilt your evening!' repeated Nan, lifting her bright eyes with the gleam of fun still in them.

'Yes,' blurted out Dick; 'why have you kept me at such a distance all the evening? Why would you not dance with me? and you gave Hamilton three valses. It was not like you, Nan, to treat me so—and on my birthday too,' went on the poor fellow, with a pathos that brought another sort of gleam to Nan's eyes, only she still laughed.

'Ah, you foolish boy!' she said, and gave his coat-sleeve a coaxing little pat. 'I would rather have danced with you than Mr. Hamilton, though he does reverse beautifully, and I never knew anyone who waltzed more perfectly.'

'Oh, I do not presume to rival Hamilton,' began Dick hotly, but she silenced him.

'Listen to me, you foolish Dick! I would have danced with you and willingly, but I knew my duty better, or rather I knew yours. You were a public man to-day; the eyes of the county were upon you. You had to pay court to the big ladies, and to take no notice of poor little me. I sent you away for your own good, and because I valued your duty above my pleasure,' continued this heroic young person, in a perfectly satisfied tone.

'And you wanted to dance with me, Nan, and not with that goose of a Hamilton?' in a wheedling voice.

'Yes, Dick; but he is not a goose for all that: he is more of a swan, in my opinion.'

'He is a conceited ass!' was the very unexpected reply, which was a little hard on Dick's chum, who was in many ways a most estimable young man, and vastly his superior. 'Why are you laughing, when you know I hate prigs? and Hamilton is about the biggest I ever knew.' But this did not mend matters, and Nan's laugh still rang merrily in the darkness.

'What are those two doing?' asked Phillis, trying to peep between the lilac-bushes, but failing to discover more than the white glimmer of Nan's shawl.

Nan's laugh, though it was full of sweet triumph, only irritated Dick; the lord of the evening was still too sore and humiliated by all these rebuffs and repulses to take the fun in good part.

'What is it that amuses you so?' he asked rather crossly; 'that is the worst of you girls, you are always so ready to make merry at a fellow's expense. You are taking Hamilton's part against me, Nan—I, who am your oldest friend, who have always been faithful to you ever since you were a child,' continued the young man, with a growing sense of aggravation.

'Oh, Dick!' and Nan's voice faltered a little; she was rather touched at this.

Dick took instant note of the change of key, and went on in the same injured voice.

'Why should I look after all the big people, and take no notice of you? Have I not made it my first duty to look after you as long as I can remember? Though the whole world were about us, would you not be the first and the principal to me?'

'Don't, Dick,' she said faintly, trying to repress him; 'you must not talk in that way, and I must not listen to you; your father would not like it.' The words were sweet to her—precious beyond everything, but she must not have him speak them. But Dick, in his angry excitement, was not to be repressed.

'What does it matter what he likes? This is between you and me, Nan; no one shall meddle between us two.' But what imprudent speech Dick was about to add was suddenly quenched in light-pealing laughter. At this critical moment they were met and surrounded;

before them was the red glow of Cathcart's cigar, the whiteness of Phillis's gown; behind were two more advancing figures. In another second the young people had joined hands—a dusky ring formed round the startled pair.

'Fairly caught!' cried Dulce's sunshiny voice; the mischievous little monkey had no idea of the sport she was spoiling. None of the young people thought of anything but fun; Dick was just Dick, and he and Nan were always together.

Dick muttered something inaudible under his breath, but Nan was quite equal to the occasion; she was still palpitating a little with the pleasure Dick's words had given her, but she confronted her tormentors boldly.

'You absurd creatures,' she said, 'to steal a march on us like that! Dick and I were having a quarrel; we were fighting so hard that we did not hear you.'

'I enjoy a good fight above everything,' exclaimed Cathcart, throwing away his cigar. He was a handsome dark-eyed boy, with no special individuality, except an overweening sense of fun. 'What's the odds, Mayne? and who is likely to be the winner?'

'Oh, Nan, of course,' returned Dick, trying to recover himself. 'I am the captive of her spear and of her bow; she is in possession of everything, myself included.'

The rest laughed at Dick's jest, as they thought it; and Mr. Hamilton said, 'Bravo, Miss Challoner! we will help to drag him at your chariot-wheels.' But Nan changed colour in the darkness.

They went in after this, and the young men took their leave in the porch. Dick's strong grip of the hand conveyed his meaning fully to Nan—'Remember I meant it all,' it seemed to say to her.

'What did it matter? I am quite sure of him—Dick is Dick,' thought Nan, as she laid her head happily on the pillow.

As for Dick, he had a long ordeal before him ere he could make his escape to the smoking-room, where his friends awaited him. Mr. Mayne had a great deal to say to him about the day, and Dick had to listen and try to look interested.

'I am sure Dick behaved beautifully,' observed Mrs. Mayne, when the son and heir had at last lounged off to his companions.

'Well, yes; he did very well on the whole,' was the grudging response; 'but I must say those Challoner girls made themselves far too conspicuous for my taste;' but to this his wife prudently made no reply.

## CHAPTER VI.

### MR. TRINDER'S VISIT.

THE next few days passed far too quickly for Nan's pleasure, and Dick's last morning arrived. The very next day the Maynes were to start for Switzerland, and Longmead was to stand empty for the remainder of the summer. It was a dreary prospect for Nan, and in spite of her high spirits her courage grew somewhat low. Six months! who could know what might happen before they met again? Nan was not the least bit superstitious, neither was it her wont to indulge in useless speculations or forebodings; but she could not shake off this morning a strange uncanny feeling that haunted her in spite of herself—

a presentiment that things were not going to be just as she would have them—that Dick and she would not meet again in exactly the same manner.

'How silly I am!' she thought for the twentieth time, as she brushed out her glossy brown hair, and arranged it in her usual simple fashion.

Nan and her sisters were a little behind the times in some ways; they had never thought fit to curl their hair *en garçon*, or to mount a pyramid of tangled curls in imitation of a poodle—no pruning scissors had touched the light-springing locks that grew so prettily about their temples; in this, as in much else, they were unlike other girls, for they dared to put individuality before fashion, and good taste and a sense of beauty against the specious arguments of the multitude.

'How silly I am!' again repeated Nan. 'What can happen, what should happen, except that I shall have a dull summer, and shall be very glad when Christmas and Dick come together;' and then Nan shook her little basket of housekeeping keys until they jingled merrily, and ran downstairs with a countenance she meant to keep bright for the rest of the day.

They were to play tennis at the Paines' that afternoon, and afterwards the three girls were to dine at Longmead. Mrs. Challoner had been invited also; but she had made some excuse, and pleaded for a quiet evening. She was never very ready to accept these invitations; there was nothing in common between her and Mrs. Mayne; and in her heart she agreed with Lady Fitzroy in thinking the master of Longmead odious.

It was Mr. Mayne who had tendered this parting hospitality to his neighbours, and he chose to be much offended at Mrs. Challoner's refusal.

'I think it is very unfriendly of your mother, when we are such old neighbours, and on our last evening too,' he said to Nan, as she entered the drawing-room that evening, bringing her mother's excuses wrapped up in the prettiest words she could find.

'Mother is not quite well; she does not feel up to the exertion of dining out to-night,' returned Nan, trying to put a good face on it, but feeling as though things were too much for her this evening. It was bad enough for Mr. Mayne to insist on them all coming up to a long formal dinner, and spoiling their chances of a twilight stroll; but it was still worse for her mother to abandon them after this fashion.

The new novel must have had something to do with this sudden indisposition; but when Mrs. Challoner had wrapped herself up in her white shawl, always a bad sign with her, and had declared herself unfit for any exertion, what could a dutiful daughter do but deliver her excuses as gracefully as she could? Nevertheless, Mr. Mayne frowned and expressed himself ill-pleased.

'I should have thought an effort could have been made on such an occasion,' was his final thrust, as he gave his arm ungraciously to Nan, and conducted her with ominous solemnity to the table.

It was not a festive meal, in spite of all Mrs. Mayne's efforts. Dick looked glum. He was separated from Nan by a vast silver épergne, that fully screened her from view. Another time she would have peeped merrily round at him, and given him a sprightly nod or two; but how was she to do it when Mr. Mayne never relaxed his gloomy muscles, and when he insisted on keeping up a ceremonious flow of conversation with her on the subjects of the day.

When Dick tried to strike into their talk, he got so visibly snubbed that he was obliged to take refuge with Phillis.

'You young fellows never know what you are talking about,' observed Mr. Mayne sharply, when Dick had hazarded a remark about the Premier's policy; 'you are a Radical one day, and a Conservative another. That comes of your debating societies. You take contrary sides, and mix up a balderdash of ideas, until you don't know whether you are standing on your head or your heels;' and it was after this that Dick found his refuge with Phillis.

It was little better when they were all in the drawing-room together. If Mr. Mayne had invited them there for the purpose of keeping them all under his own eyes and making them uncomfortable, he could not have managed better. When Dick suggested a stroll in the garden, he said:

'Pshaw! what nonsense proposing such a thing, when the dews are heavy and the girls will catch their deaths of cold!'

'We do it every evening of our life,' observed Nan hardily; but even she dare not persevere in the face of this protest, though she exchanged a rebellious look with Dick that did him good, and put him in a better humour.

They found their way into the conservatory after that, but were hunted out on pretence of having a little music; at least, Nan would have it that it was pretence.

'Your father does not care much for music, I know,' she whispered, as she placed herself at the grand piano, while Dick leant against it and watched her. It was naughty of Nan, but there was no denying that she found Mr. Mayne more aggravating than usual this evening.

'Come, come, Miss Nancy!' he called out—he always called her that when he wished to annoy her, for Nan had a special dislike to her quaint, old-fashioned name; it had been her mother's and grandmother's name; in every generation there had been a Nancy

Challoner—'Come, come, Miss Nancy! we cannot have you playing at hide-and-seek in this fashion. We want some music; give us something rousing, to keep us all awake;' and Nan had reluctantly placed herself at the piano.

She did her little best according to orders, for she dare not offend Dick's father. None of the Challoners were accomplished girls. Dulce sang a little, and so did Nan, but Phillis could not play the simplest piece without bungling; and her uncertain little warblings, which were sweet but hardly true, were reserved for church.

Dulce sang very prettily, but she could only manage her own accompaniments or a sprightly valse. Nan, who did most of the execution of the family, was a very fair performer from a young lady's point of view, and that is not saying much. She always had her piece ready if people wanted her to play. She sat down without nervousness and rose without haste. She had a choice little repertoire of old songs and ballads, that she could produce without hesitation from memory. 'My mother bids me bind my hair,' or 'Bid your faithful Ariel fly,' and such-like old songs, in which there is more melody than in a hundred new ones, and which she sang in a simple, artless fashion that pleased the elder people greatly.

Dulce could do more than this, but her voice had never been properly tutored, and she sang her bird-music in bird-fashion, rather wildly and shrilly, with small respect to rule and art, nevertheless making a pleasing noise, as a young foreigner once told her.

When Nan had exhausted her little stock, Mr. Mayne peremptorily invited them to a round game; and the rest of the evening was spent in trying to master the mysteries of a new game, over the involved rules of which Mr. Mayne, as usual, wrangled fiercely with everybody, while Dick shrugged his shoulders and shuffled his cards with such evident ill-humour, that Nan hurried her sisters away half an hour before the usual time, in terror of an outbreak.

It was an utterly disappointing evening; and to make matters worse, Mr. Mayne actually lit his cigar and strolled down the garden-paths, keeping quite close to Nan, and showing such obvious intention of accompanying them to the very gate of the cottage, that there could be no thought of any sweet lingering in the dusk.

'I will be even with him,' growled Dick, who was in a state of suppressed irritation under this unexpected surveillance; and in the darkest part of the road he twitched Nan's sleeve to attract her attention, and whispered in so low a voice that his father could not hear him: 'This is not good-bye. I will be round at the cottage to-morrow morning;' and Nan nodded hurriedly, and then turned her head to answer Mr. Mayne's last question.

If Dick had put all his feelings in his hand-shake, it could not have spoken to Nan more eloquently of the young man's wrath and chagrin and concealed tenderness. Nan shot him one of her swift straightforward looks in answer.

'Never mind,' it seemed to say, 'we shall have to-morrow;' and then she bade them cheerfully good-night.

Dorothy met her in the hall, and put down her chamber-candlestick.

'Has the mother gone to bed yet, Dorothy?'

questioned the young mistress, speaking still with that enforced cheerfulness.

'No, Miss Nan; she is still in there,' jerking her head in the direction of the drawing-room. 'Mr. Trinder called, and was with her a long time. I thought she seemed a bit poorly when I took in the lamp.'

'Mamsie is never fit for anything when that old ogre has been,' broke in Dulce impatiently. 'He always comes and tells her some nightmare tale or other to prevent her sleeping. Now we shall not have the new gowns we set our hearts on, Nan.'

'Oh, never mind the gowns,' returned Nan, rather wearily.

What did it matter if they had to wear their old ones when Dick would not be there to see them? and Dorothy, who was contemplating her favourite nursling with the privileged tenderness of an old servant, chimed in with the utmost cheerfulness.

'It does not matter what she wears—does it, Miss Nan? She looks just as nice in an old gown as a new one; that is what I say of all my young ladies—dress does not matter a bit to them.'

'How long are you all going to stand chattering with Dorothy?' interrupted Phillis, in her clear decided voice. 'Mother will wonder what conspiracy we are hatching, and why we leave her so long alone.' And then Dorothy took up her candlestick, grumbling a little, as she often did, over Miss Phillis's masterful ways, and the girls went laughingly into their mother's presence.

Though it was summer-time, Mrs. Challoner's easy-chair was drawn up in front of the rug, and she sat wrapped in her white shawl, with her eyes fixed on the pretty painted fire-screen that hid the blackness of the coals. She did not turn her head or move as her daughters entered; indeed, so motionless was her attitude that Dulce thought she was asleep, and went on tiptoe round her chair to steal a kiss. But Nan, who had caught sight of her mother's face, put her quickly aside.

'Don't, Dulce; mother is not well. What is the matter, mammie darling?' kneeling down and bringing her bright face on a level with her mother's. She would have taken her into her vigorous young arms, but Mrs. Challoner almost pushed her away.

'Hush, children! Do be quiet, Nan; I cannot talk to you. I cannot answer questions to-night.' And then she shivered and drew her shawl closer round her, and put away Nan's caressing hands, and looked at them all with a face that seemed to have grown pinched and old all at once, and eyes full of misery.

'Mammie, you must speak to us,' returned Nan, not a whit daunted by this rebuff, but horribly frightened all the time. 'Of course Dorothy told us that Mr. Trinder has been here, and of course we know that it is some trouble about money;' then, at the mention of Mr. Trinder's name, Mrs. Challoner shivered again.

Nan waited a moment for an answer; but as none came, she went on in a coaxing voice.

'Don't be afraid to tell us, mother darling; we can all bear a little trouble, I hope. We have had such happy lives, and we cannot go on being happy always,' continued the girl, with the painful conviction coming suddenly into her mind that the brightness of these days were over. 'Money is very nice, and one cannot do without it, I suppose; but as long as we are together and love each other——'

Then Mrs. Challoner fixed her heavy eyes on her daughter, and took up the unfinished sentence :

'Ah, if we could only be together—if I were not to be separated from my children ! it is that—that is crushing me !' and then she pressed her dry lips together, and folded her hands with a gesture of despair ; ' but I know that it must be, for Mr. Trinder has told me everything. It is no use shutting our eyes and struggling on any longer, for we are ruined—ruined !' her voice sinking into indistinctness.

Nan grew a little pale. If they were ruined, how would it be with her and Dick ? And then she thought of Mr. Mayne, and her heart felt faint within her. Nan, who had Dick added to her perplexities, was hardly equal to the emergency ; but it was Phillis who took the domestic helm as it fell from her sister's hand.

' If we be ruined, mother,' she said briskly, ' it is not half so bad as having you ill. Nan, why don't you rub her hands ? she is shivering with cold, or with the bad news, or something. I mean to set Dorothy at defiance, and to light a nice little fire, in spite of the clean muslin curtains. When one is ill or unhappy there is nothing so soothing as a fire,' continued Phillis, as she removed the screen and kindled the dry wood, not heeding Mrs. Challoner's feeble remonstrances.

'Don't, Phillis; we shall not be able to afford fires now;' and then she became a little hysterical. But Phillis persisted, and the red glow was soon coaxed into a cheerful blaze.

'That looks more comfortable. I feel chilly myself—these summer nights are sometimes deceptive. I wonder what Dorothy will say to us; I mean to ask her to make us all some tea. No, mammy, you are not to interfere; it will do you good, and we don't mean to have you ill if we can help it.' And then she looked meaningly at Nan, and withdrew.

There was no boiling water of course, and the kitchen fire was raked out; and Dorothy was sitting in solitary state, looking very grim.

'It is time for folks to be in their beds, Miss Phillis,' she said very crossly. 'I don't hold with tea myself so late; it excites people, and keeps them awake.'

'Mother is not just the thing, and a cup of tea will do her good; don't let us keep you up, Dorothy,' replied Phillis blandly. 'I have lighted the drawing-room fire, and I can boil the kettle in there. If mother has got a chill, I would not answer for the consequences.'

Dorothy grew huffy at the mention of the fire, and would not aid or abet her young lady's 'fad,' as she called it.

'If you don't want me, I think I will go to bed, Miss Phillis. Susan went off a long time ago.' And as Phillis cheerfully acquiesced in this arrangement, Dorothy decamped with a frown on her brow, and left Phillis mistress of the situation.

'There now, I have got rid of the cross old thing,' she observed in a tone of relief, as she filled the kettle and arranged the little tea-tray.

She carried them both into the room, poising the tray skilfully in her hand. Nan looked up in a relieved way as she entered. Mrs. Challoner was stretching out her chilled hands to the blaze. Her face had lost its pinched unnatural expression; it was as though the presence of her girls fenced her in securely, and her misfortune grew more shadowy and faded into the background. She drank the tea when it was given to her, and even begged Nan to follow her example. Nan took a little to please her, though she hardly believed its solace would be great; but Phillis and Dulce drank theirs in a business-like way, as though they needed support and were not ashamed to own it. It was Nan who put down her cup first, and leaned her cheek against her mother's hand.

'Now, mother dear, we want to hear all about it. Does Mr. Trinder say we are really so dreadfully poor?'

'We have been getting poorer for a long time,' returned her mother mournfully; 'but if we had only a little left us I would not complain. You see, your father would persist in these investments in spite of all Mr. Trinder could say, and now his words have come true.' But this vague statement did not satisfy Nan; and patiently, and with difficulty, she drew from her mother all that the lawyer had told her.

Mr. Challoner had been called to the Bar early in life, but his career had hardly been a successful one. He had held few briefs, and though he worked hard, and had good capabilities, he had never achieved fortune; and as he lived up to his income, and was rather fond of the good things of this life, he got through most of his wife's money, and, contrary to the advice of older and wiser heads, invested the remainder in the business of a connection who only wanted capital to make his fortune and Mr. Challoner's too.

It was a grievous error; and yet if Mr. Challoner had lived, those few thousands would hardly have been so sorely missed. He was young in his profession, and if he had been spared, success would have come to him as to other men; but he was cut off unexpectedly in the prime of life, and Mrs. Challoner gave up her large house at Kensington, and settled at Glen Cottage with her three daughters, understanding that life was changed for her, and that they must have to be content with small means and few wants.

Hitherto they had had sufficient; but of late there had been dark whispers concerning that invested money: things were not quite square and above-board; the integrity of the firm was doubted. Mr. Trinder, almost with tears in his eyes, begged Mrs. Challoner to be prudent and spend less. The crash which he had foreseen, and had vainly tried to avert, had come to-night. Gardiner and Fowler were bankrupt, and their greatest creditor, Mrs. Challoner, was ruined.

'We cannot get our money. Mr. Trinder says we never shall. They have been paying their dividends correctly, keeping it up as a sort of blind, he says; but all the capital is eaten away. George Gardiner too, your father's cousin, the man he trusted above everyone—he, to defraud the widow and the fatherless, to take our money—my children's only portion—and to leave us beggared;' and Mrs. Challoner, made tragical by this great blow, clasped her hands and looked at her girls with two large tears rolling down her face.

'Mother, are you sure? is it quite as bad as that?' asked Nan; and then she kissed away the tears, and said something rather brokenly about having faith, and trying not to lose courage; then her voice failed her, and they all sat quiet together.

## CHAPTER VII.

#### PHILLIS'S CATECHISM.

A VEIL of silence fell over the little party. After the first few moments of dismay, conjecture and exclamation, there did not seem to be much that anyone could say. Each girl was busy with her own thoughts and private interpretation of a most sorrowful enigma. What were they to do? How were they to live without separation, and without taking a solitary plunge into an unknown and most terrifying world?

Nan's frame of mind was slightly monotonous. What would Dick say, and how would this affect certain vague hopes she had lately cherished? Then she thought of Mr. Mayne and shivered, and a sense of coldness and remote fears stole over her.

One could hardly blame her for this sweet dual selfishness, that was not selfishness. She was thinking less of herself than of a certain vigorous young life that was becoming strongly entwined with hers. It was all very well to say Dick was Dick; but what could the most obstinate will of even that most obstinate young man avail against such a miserable combination of adverse influences—'when the stars in their courses fought against Sisera'? And at this juncture of her thoughts she could feel Phillis's hand folding softly over hers with a most sisterly pressure of full understanding and sympathy. Phillis had no Dick to stand sentinel over her private thoughts; she was free to be alert and vigilant for others. Nevertheless, her forehead was puckered up with hard thinking, and her silence was so very expressive that Dulce sat and looked at her with grave unsmiling eyes, the innocent child-look in them growing very pathetic at the speechlessness that had overtaken them. As for Mrs. Challoner, she still moaned feebly from time to time, as she stretched her numb hands towards the comforting warmth. They were fine delicate hands with the polished look of old ivory, and there were diamond rings on them that twinkled and shone as she moved them in her restlessness.

'They shall all go; I will keep nothing,' she said, regarding them plaintively; for they were heirlooms, and highly valued as relics of a 'wealthy past.' 'It is not this sort of thing that I mind. I would live on a crust thankfully, if I could only keep my children with me;' and she looked round at the blooming faces of her girls with eyes brimming over with maternal fondness.

Poor Dulce's lip quivered, and she made a horrified gesture.

'Oh, mamsie, don't talk so! I never could bear crusts, unless they were well buttered. I like everything to be nice, and to have plenty of it—plenty of sunshine, and fun, and holiday-making, and friends; and— and now you are talking as though we must starve, and never have anything to wear, and go nowhere, and be miserable for ever.' And here Dulce broke into actual sobs; for was she not the petted darling? and had she not had a life so gilded by sunshine, that she had never seen the dark edge of a single cloud? So that even Nan forgot Dick for a moment, and looked at her young sister pityingly; but Phillis interposed with bracing severity.

'Don't talk such nonsense, Dulce. Of course we must eat to live, and of course we must have clothes to wear. Aren't Nan and I thinking ourselves into headaches by trying to contrive how even the crusts you so despise are to be bought?' which was hardly true, as far as Nan was concerned; for she blushed guiltily over this telling point in Phillis's eloquence. 'It only upsets mother to talk like this;' and then she touched the coals skilfully, till they spluttered and blazed into fury. 'There is the Friary, you know,' she continued, looking calmly round on them, as though she felt herself full of resources. 'If Dulce chooses to make herself miserable about the crusts, we have, at least, a roof to shelter us.'

'I forgot the Friary,' murmured Nan, looking at her sister with admiration; and, though Mrs. Challoner said nothing, she started a little as though she had forgotten it too. But Dulce was not to be comforted.

'That horrid, dismal, pokey old cottage!' she returned, with a shrill rendering of each adjective. 'You would have us go and live in that damp, musty, fusty place?'

Phillis gave a succession of quick little nods.

'I don't think it particularly dismal, or Nan either,' she returned, in her brisk way. Phillis always answered for Nan, and was never contradicted. 'It is not dear Glen Cottage, of course; but we could not begin munching our crusts here,' she continued, with a certain grim humour. Things were apparently at their worst; but at least she —Phillis—the clever one, as she had heard herself called, would do her best to keep the heads of the little family above water. 'It is a nice little place enough, if we were only humble enough to see it; and it is not damp, and it is our own,' running up the advantages as well as she could.

'The Friary!' commented her mother in some surprise; 'to think of that queer old cottage coming into your head! And it so seldom lets. And people say it is dear at forty pounds a year; and it is so dull, that they do not care to stay.'

'Never mind all that, mammy,' returned Phillis, with a grave business-like face. 'A cottage, rent free, that will hold us, is not to be despised; and Hadleigh is a nice place, and the sea always suits you. There is the house and the furniture, that belongs to us; and we have plenty of clothes for the present. How much did Mr. Trinder think we should have in hand?'

Then her mother told her, but still mournfully, that they might possibly have about a hundred pounds. 'But there are my rings, and that piece of point-lace that Lady Fitzroy admires so——' but Phillis waved away that proposition with an impatient frown.

'There is plenty of time for that when we have got through all the money; not that a hundred pounds would last long, with moving, and paying off the servants, and all that sort of thing.'

Then Nan, who had worn all along an expression of admiring confidence in Phillis's resources, originated an idea of her own.

'The mother might write to uncle Francis, perhaps;' but at this proposition Mrs. Challoner sat upright, and looked almost offended.

'My dear Nan, what a preposterous idea! Your uncle Francis!'

'Well, mammy, he is our uncle; and I am sure he would be sorry if his only brother's children were to starve.'

'You are too young to know any better,' returned Mrs. Challoner, relapsing into alarmed feebleness; 'you are not able to judge. But I never liked my brother-in-law—never; he was not a good man. He was not a person whom one could trust,' continued the poor lady, trying to soften down certain facts to her innocent young daughters.

Sir Francis Challoner had been a black sheep—a very black sheep indeed: one who had dyed himself certainly to a most sable hue; and though, for such prodigals, there may be a late repentance and much killing of fatted calves, still Mrs. Challoner was right in refusing to entrust herself and her children to the uncertain mercies of such a sinner.

Now Nan knew nothing about the sin; but she did think that an uncle who was a baronet threw a certain reflected glory or brightness over them. Sir Francis might be that very suspicious character — a black sheep; he might be landless, with the exception of that ruined tenement in the north; nevertheless, Nan loved to know that he was of their kith and kin. It seemed to settle their claims to respectability, and held Mr. Mayne in some degree of awe; and he knew that his own progenitors had not the faintest trace of blue blood, and numbered more aldermen than baronets.

It would have surprised and grieved Nan, especially just now, if she had known that no such glory remained to her—that Sir Francis Challoner had long filled the cup of his iniquities, and lay in his wife's tomb in some distant cemetery, leaving a certain red-headed Sir Harry to reign in his stead.

'I don't think we had better talk any more,' observed Phillis somewhat brusquely; and then she exchanged meaning looks with Nan. The two girls were somewhat dismayed at their mother's wan looks; her feebleness and uncertainty of speech, the very vagueness of her lamentations filled them with sad forebodings for the future. How were they to leave her, when they commenced that little fight with the world? She had leaned on them so long that her helplessness had become a matter of habit.

Nan understood her sister's warning glance, and she made no further allusion to Sir Francis; she only rose with assumed briskness, and took her mother in charge.

'Now I am going to help you to bed, mammy darling,' she said cheerfully. 'Phillis is quite right, we will not talk any more to-night; we shall want all our strength for to-morrow. We will just say our prayers, and try and go to sleep, and hope that things may turn out better than we expect;' and as Mrs. Challoner was too utterly spent to resist this wise counsel, Nan achieved her pious mission with some success. She sat down by the bedside and leaned her head against her mother's pillow, and soon had the satisfaction of hearing the even breathing that proved that the sleeper had forgotten her troubles for a little while.

'Poor dear mother, how exhausted she must have been!' thought Nan, as she closed the door softly. She was far too anxious and wide awake herself to dream of retiring to rest. She was somewhat surprised to find her sisters' room dark and empty as she passed. They must be still downstairs talking over things in the firelight; they were as little inclined for sleep as she was. Phillis's carefully decocted tea must have stimulated them to wakefulness.

The room was still bright with firelight. Dulce was curled up in her mother's chair, and had evidently been indulging in what she called 'a good cry.' Phillis, sombre and thoughtful, was pacing the room with her hands clasped behind her head, a favourite attitude of hers when she was in any perplexity. She stopped short as Nan regarded her with some astonishment from the threshold.

'Oh, come in Nan; it will be such a relief to talk to a sensible person. Dulce is so silly, she does nothing but cry.'

'I can't help it,' returned Dulce, with another sob; 'everything is so horrible, and Phillis will say such dreadful things.'

'Poor little soul!' said Nan, in a sympathetic voice, sitting down on the arm of the chair and stroking Dulce's hair; 'it is very hard for her, and for us all,' with a pent-up sigh.

'Of course it is hard,' retorted Phillis, confronting them rather impatiently from the hearthrug; 'it is bitterly hard. But it is not worse for Dulce than for the rest of us. Crying will not mend matters, and it is a sheer waste of tears. As I tell her, what we have to do now is to make the best of things, and see what is to be done under the circumstances.'

'Yes indeed,' repeated Nan meekly; but she put her arm round Dulce, and drew her head against her shoulder. The action comforted Dulce, and her tears soon ceased to flow.

'I am thinking about mother,' went on Phillis, pondering her words slowly as she spoke; 'she does look so ill and weak. I do not see how we are to leave her.'

Mrs. Challoner's moral helplessness and dread of responsibility were so sacred in her daughters' eyes that they rarely alluded to it except in this vague fashion. For years they had shielded and petted her, and given way to her little fads and fancies, until she had developed into a sort of gentle hypochondriac.

'Mother cannot bear this; we always keep these little worries from her,' Nan had been accustomed to say; and the others had followed her example.

The unspoken thought lay heavy upon them now. How were they to prevent the rough winds of adversity from blowing too roughly upon their cherished charge? The roof, and perhaps the crust, might be theirs; but how were they to contrive that she should not miss her little comforts? They would gladly work, but how, and after what fashion?

Phillis was the first to plunge into the unwelcome topic, for Nan felt almost as helpless and bewildered as Dulce.

'We must go into the thing thoroughly,' began Phillis, drawing a chair opposite to her sisters. She was very pale, but her eyes had a certain brightness of determination. She looked too young for that quiet careworn look that had come so suddenly to her; but one felt she could be equal to any emergency. 'We are down-hearted, of course; but we have plenty of time for all that sort of thing. The question is, how are we to live?'

'Just so,' observed Nan, rather dubiously; and Dulce gave a little gasp.

'There is the Friary standing empty; and there is the furniture; and there will be about fifty pounds, perhaps less, when everything is settled. And we have clothes enough to last some time, and——' here Dulce put her hands together pleadingly, but Phillis looked at her severely, and went on: 'Forty or fifty pounds will soon be spent, and then we shall be absolutely penniless; we have no one to help us. Mother will not hear of writing to uncle Francis: we must work ourselves, or starve.'

'Couldn't we let lodgings?' hazarded Dulce, with quavering voice; but Phillis smiled grimly.

'Let lodgings at the Friary! why, it is only big enough to hold us. We might get a larger house in Hadleigh; but no, it would be ruinous to fail, and perhaps we should not make it answer. I cannot fancy mother living in the basement story; she would make herself wretched over it. We are too young.

I don't think that would answer, Nan; do you?'

Nan replied faintly that she did not think it would. The mere proposition took her breath away. What would Mr. Mayne say to that? Then she plucked up spirit and went into the question vigorously.

There were too many lodging-houses in Hadleigh now; it would be a hazardous speculation, and one likely to fail; they had not sufficient furniture for such a purpose, and they dare not use up their little capital too quickly. They were too young, too, to carry out such a thing. Nan did not add, 'and too pretty,' though she coloured and hesitated here. Their mother could not help them; she was not strong enough for housework or cooking. She thought that plan must be given up.

'We might be daily governesses, and live at home,' suggested Dulce, who found a sort of relief in throwing out feelers in every direction. Nan brightened up visibly at this, but Phillis's moody brow did not relax for a moment.

'That would be nice,' acquiesced Nan, 'and then mother would not find the day so long if we came home in the evening; she could busy herself about the house, and we could leave her little things to do, and she would not find the hours so heavy. I like that idea of yours, Dulce; and we are all so fond of children.'

'The idea is as nice as possible,' replied Phillis, with an ominous stress on the noun, 'if we could only make it practicable.'

'Phil is going to find fault,' pouted Dulce, who knew every inflection of Phillis's voice.

'Oh dear no, nothing of the kind!' she retorted briskly. 'Nan is quite right—we all doat on children. I should dearly like to be a governess myself—it would be more play than work; but I am only wondering who would engage us.'

'Who?—oh, anybody!' returned Nan, feeling puzzled by the smothered satire of Phillis's speech. 'Of course we are not certificated, and I for one could only teach young children; but——' here Phillis interrupted her.

'Don't think me horrid if I ask you and Dulce some questions, but do—do answer me just as though I were going through the Catechism: we are only girls, but we must sift the whole thing thoroughly. Are we fit for governesses? what can you and I and Dulce teach?'

'Oh, anything!' returned Nan, still more vaguely.

'My dear Nanny, anything won't do. Come, I am really in earnest; I mean to catechize you both thoroughly.'

'Very well,' returned Nan, in a resigned voice; but Dulce looked a little frightened. As for Phillis, she sat erect, with her finger pointed at them in a severely ominous fashion.

'How about history, Nan? I thought you could never remember dates; you used to jumble facts in the most marvellous manner. I remember your insisting that Anne of Cleves was Louis XII.'s second wife; and you shocked Miss Martin dreadfully by declaring that one of Marlborough's victories was fought at Cressy.'

'I never could remember historical facts,' returned Nan humbly. 'Dulce always did better than I; and so did you, Phillis. When I teach the children I can have the book before me.' But Phillis only shook her head at this, and went on:

'Dulce was a shade better, but I don't believe she could tell me the names of the English sovereigns in proper sequence;' but Dulce disdained to answer. 'You were better at arithmetic, Nan. Dulce never got through her rule of three; but you were not very advanced even at that. You write a pretty hand, and you used to talk French very fluently.'

'Oh, I have forgotten my French!' exclaimed Nan, in a panic-stricken voice. 'Dulce, don't you remember we quite settled to talk in French over our work three times a week, and we have always forgotten it; and we were reading Madame de Sévigné's "Letters" together, and I found the book the other day quite covered with dust.'

'I hate French,' returned Dulce rebelliously. 'I began German with Phillis, and like it much better.'

'True, but we are only beginners,' returned the remorseless Phillis; 'it was very nice, of course, and the "Taugenichts" was delicious; but think how many words in every sentence you had to hunt out in the dictionary. I am glad you feel so competent, Dulce; but I could not teach German myself, or French either. I don't remember enough of the grammar; and I do not believe Nan does either, though she used to chatter so to Miss Martin.'

'Did I not say she would pick our idea to pieces?' returned Dulce, with tears in her eyes.

'My dear little sister, don't look so dreadfully pathetic. I am quite as disheartened and disappointed as you are. Nan says she has forgotten her French, and she will have to teach history with an open book before her; we none of us draw—no, Dulce, please let me finish our scanty stock of accomplishments. I only know my notes—for no one cares to hear me lumber through my pieces—and I sing at church. You have the sweetest voice, Dulce, but it is not trained; and I cannot compliment you on your playing. Nan sings and plays very nicely, and it is a pleasure to listen to her; but I am afraid she knows little about the theory of music, harmony and thorough-bass—you never did anything in that way, did you, Nan?'

Nan shook her head sadly. She was too discomfited for speech. Phillis looked at them both thoughtfully; her trouble was very real, but she could not help a triumphant inflection in her voice.

'Dear Nan, please do not look so unhappy. Dulce, you shall not begin to cry again. Don't you remember what mother was reading to us the other day, about the country being flooded with incompetent governesses—half-educated girls turned loose on the world to earn their living? I can remember one sentence of that writer, word for word. "The standard of education is so high at the present day, and the number of certificated reliable teachers so much increased, that we can afford to discourage the crude efforts to teach, or un-teach, our children." And then he goes on to ask, "What has become of womanly conscientiousness, when such ignorance presses forward to assume such sacred responsibilities? Better the competent nurse than the incompetent governess." "Why do not these girls," he asks, "who, through their own fault or the fault of circumstances, are not sufficiently advanced to educate others—why do they not rather discharge the exquisitely feminine duties of the nursery? What an advantage to parents to have their little ones brought into the earliest contact with refined speech and cultivated manners—their infant ears not inoculated by barbarous English!"' but here Phillis was arrested in her torrent of reflected wisdom by an impatient exclamation from Dulce.

'Oh, Nan, do ask her to be quiet! She never stops when she once begins. How can we listen to such rubbish, when we are so wretched? You may talk for hours, Phil, but I never, never will be a nurse!' and Dulce hid her face on Nan's shoulder in such undisguised distress, that her sisters had much ado to comfort her.

## CHAPTER VIII.

'WE SHOULD HAVE TO CARRY PARCELS.'

IT was hard work to tranquillize Dulce.

'I never, never will be a nurse,' she sobbed out at intervals.

'You little goose, who ever thought of such a thing? Why will you misunderstand me so?' sighed Phillis, almost in despair at her sister's impracticability. 'I am only trying to prove to you and Nan that we are not fit for governesses.'

'No, indeed; I fear you are right there,' replied poor Nan, who had never realized her deficiencies before. They were all bright, taking girls, with plenty to say for themselves; ladylike, and well-bred. Who would have thought that, when weighed in the balance, they would have been found so wanting? 'I always knew I was a very stupid person; but you are different—you are so clever, Phil.'

'Nonsense, Nanny! it is a sort of cleverness for which there is no market. I am fond of reading. I remember things, and do a great deal of thinking; but I am destitute of accomplishments—my knowledge of languages is purely superficial. We are equal to other girls—just young ladies, and nothing more; but when it comes to earning our bread-and-butter——' Here Phillis paused, and threw out her hands with a little gesture of despair.

'But you work so beautifully; and so does Nan,' interrupted Dulce, who was a little comforted now she knew Phillis had no prospective nursemaid theory in view. 'I am good at it myself,' she continued modestly, feeling, in this case, self-praise was allowable. 'We might be companions—some nice old lady who wants her caps made, and requires some one to read to her,' faltered Dulce, with her childlike pleading look.

Nan gave her a little hug; but she left the answer to Phillis, who went at once into a brown study, and only woke up after a long interval.

'I am looking at it all round,' she said, when Nan at last pressed for her opinion; 'it is not a bad idea. I think it very possible that either you or I, Nan—or both, perhaps—might find something in that line to suit us. There are old ladies everywhere; and some of them are rich and lonely, and want companions.'

'You have forgotten me!' exclaimed Dulce, with natural jealousy, and a dislike to be overlooked, inherent in most young people. 'And it is I who have always made mammy's caps; and you know how Lady Fitzroy praised the last one.'

'Yes, yes; we know all that,' returned Phillis impatiently. 'You are as clever as possible with your fingers; but one of us must stop with mother, and you are the youngest, Dulce—that is what I meant by looking at it all round. If Nan and I were away, it would never do for you and mother to live at the Friary. We could not afford a servant, and we should want the forty pounds a year to pay for bare necessaries; for our salary would not be very great. You would have to live in lodgings—two little rooms, that is all; and even then I am afraid you and mother would be dreadfully pinched, for we should have to dress ourselves properly in other people's houses.'

'Oh, Phillis, that would not do at all!' exclaimed Nan, in a voice of despair. She was very pale by this time: full realization of all this trouble was coming to her, as it had to Phillis. 'What shall we do? Who will help us to any decision? How are you and I to go away and live luxuriously in other people's houses, and leave mother and Dulce pining in two shabby little rooms, with nothing to do, and perhaps not enough to eat, and mother fretting herself ill, and Dulce losing her bloom? I could not rest; I could not sleep for thinking of it. I would rather take in plain needlework, and live on dry bread, if we could only be together, and help each other.'

'So would I,' returned Phillis, in an odd, muffled voice.

'And I too,' rather hesitatingly from Dulce.

'If we could only live at the Friary, and have Dorothy to do all the rough work,' sighed Nan, with a sudden yearning towards even that very shabby ark of refuge; 'if we could only be together, and see each other every day, things would not be quite so dreadful.'

'I am quite of your opinion,' was Phillis's curt observation; but there was a sudden gleam in her eyes.

'I have heard of ladies working for fancy-shops—do you think we could do something of that kind?' asked Nan anxiously. 'Even mother could help us in that; and Dulce does work so beautifully. It is all very well to say we have no accomplishments,' went on Nan, with a pathetic little laugh; 'but you know that no other girls work as we do. We have always made our own dresses. And Lady Fitzroy asked me once who was our dressmaker, because she fitted us so exquisitely; and I was so proud of telling her that we always did our own, with Dorothy to help——'

'Nan,' interrupted Phillis eagerly; and there was a great softness in her whole mien, and her eyes were glistening. 'Dear Nan, do you love us all so that you could give the whole world for our sakes—for the sake of living together, I mean?'

Nan hesitated. Did the whole world involve Dick, and could even her love for her sisters induce her voluntarily to give him up? Phillis, who was quick-witted, read the doubt in a moment, and hastened to qualify her words.

'The outside world, I mean—mere conventional acquaintances, not friends. Do you think you could bear to set society at defiance, to submit to be sent to Coventry for our sakes; to do without it in fact, to live in a little world of our own and make ourselves happy in it?'

'Ah, Phillis, you are so clever, and I don't understand you,' faltered Nan. It was not Dick she was to give up; but what could Phillis mean? 'We are all fond of society; we are like other girls, I suppose. But if we are to be poor and work for our living, I dare say people will give us up.'

'I am not meaning that,' returned her

sister earnestly; 'it is something far harder, something far more difficult, something that will be a great sacrifice and cost us all tremendous efforts. But if we are to keep a roof over our heads, if we are to live together in anything like comfort, I don't see what else we can do, unless we go out as companions, and leave mother and Dulce in lodgings.'

'Oh, no, no; pray don't leave us!' implored Dulce, feeling all her strength and comfort lay near Nan.

'I will not leave you, dear, if I can possibly help it,' returned Nan gently. 'Tell us what you mean, Phillis, for I see you have some sort of plan in your head. There is nothing—nothing,' she continued more firmly, 'that I would not do to make mother and Dulce happy. Speak out; you are half afraid that I shall prove a coward, but you shall see.'

'Dear Nan, no; you are as brave as possible. I am rather a coward myself. Yes, I have a plan; but you have yourself put it into my head by saying what you did about Lady Fitzroy.'

'About Lady Fitzroy?'

'Yes; your telling her about our making our own dresses. Nan, you are right; needlework is our forte; nothing is a trouble to us. Few girls have such clever fingers, I believe; and then you and Dulce have such taste. Mrs. Paine once told me that we were the best-dressed girls in the neighbourhood, and she wished Carrie looked half as well. I am telling you this, not from vanity, but because I do believe we can turn our one talent to account. We should be miserable governesses; we do not want to separate and seek situations as lady helps or companions; we do not mean to fail in letting lodgings—but if we do not succeed as good dressmakers, never believe me again.'

'Dressmakers!' almost shrieked Dulce. But Nan, who had expressed herself willing to take in plain needlework, only looked at her sister with mute gravity; her little world was turned so completely upside down, everything was so unreal, that nothing at this moment could have surprised her.

'Dressmakers!' she repeated vaguely.

'Yes, yes,' replied Phillis, still more eagerly. The inspiration had come to her in a moment, full-fledged and grown-up, like Minerva from the head of Jupiter. Just from those chance words of Nan's she had grasped the whole thing in a moment. Now, indeed, she felt that she was clever; here at least was something striking and original; she took no notice of Dulce's shocked exclamation; she fixed her eyes solemnly on Nan. 'Yes, yes; what does it matter what the outside world says? We are not like other girls—we never were; people always said we were so original. Necessity strikes out strange paths sometimes. We could not do such a thing here—no, no, I never could submit to that myself,' as Nan involuntarily shuddered; 'but at Hadleigh, where no one knows us, where we shall be among strangers. And then, you see, Miss Monks is dead.'

'Oh dear—oh dear! what does she mean?' cried Dulce despairingly; 'and what do we care about Miss Monks, if the creature be dead—or about Miss Anybody, if we have got to do such dreadful things?'

'My dear,' returned Phillis, with compassionate irony, 'if we had to depend upon you for ideas——' and here she made an eloquent pause. 'Our last tenant for the Friary was Miss Monks, and Miss Monks was a dressmaker; and though perhaps I ought not to say it, it does seem a direct leading of Providence, putting such a thought into my head.'

'I am afraid Dulce and I are very slow and stupid,' returned Nan, putting her hair rather wearily from her face; her pretty colour had quite faded during the last half-hour. 'I think if you would tell us plainly, exactly what you mean, Phillis, we should be able to understand everything better.'

'My notion is this,' began Phillis slowly; 'remember, I have not thought it quite out, but I will give you my ideas just as they occur to me. We will not say anything to mother just yet, until we have thoroughly digested our plan. You and I, Nan, will run down to the Friary and reconnoitre the place, judge of its capabilities, and so forth; and when we come back we will hold a family council.'

'That will be best,' agreed Nan, who remembered, with sudden feelings of relief, that Dick and his belongings would be safe in the Engadine by that time. 'But, Phillis, do you really and truly believe that we could carry out such a scheme?'

'Why not?' was the bold answer. 'If we can work for ourselves, we can for other people. I have a presentiment that we shall achieve a striking success. We will make the old Friary as comfortable as possible,' she continued cheerfully. 'The good folk of Hadleigh will be rather surprised when they see our pretty rooms. No horse-hair sofa; no crochet antimacassars or hideous wax-flowers—none of the usual stock-in-trade. Dorothy will manage the house for us; and we will all sit and work together, and mother will help us, and read to us. Aren't you glad, Nan, that we all saved up for that splendid sewing-machine?'

'I do believe there is something after all in what you say,' was Nan's response; but Dulce was not so easily won over.

'Do you mean to say that we shall put up a brass plate on the door, with "Challoner, dressmaker," on it?' she observed indignantly. A red glow mounted to Nan's forehead; and even Phillis looked disconcerted.

'I never thought of that—well, perhaps

not. We might advertise at the Library, or put cards in the shops. I do not think mother would ever cross the threshold if she saw a brass plate.'

'No, no; I could not bear that,' said Nan faintly. A dim vision of Dick standing at the gate, ruefully contemplating their name —her name—in juxtaposition with 'dressmaker,' crossed her mind directly.

'But we should have to carry parcels, and stand in people's halls, and perhaps fit Mrs. Squails, the grocer's wife—that fat old thing, you know. How would you like to make a dress for Mrs. Squails, Phil?' asked Dulce, with the malevolent desire of making Phillis as uncomfortable as possible; but Phillis, who had rallied from her momentary discomfiture, was not to be again worsted.

'Dulce, you talk like a child; you are really a very silly little thing. Do you think any work can degrade us, or that we shall not be as much gentlewomen at Hadleigh as we are here?'

'But the parcels?' persisted Dulce.

'I do not intend to carry any,' was the imperturbable reply. 'Dorothy will do that;

or we will hire a boy. As for waiting in halls, I don't think anyone will ask me to do that, as I should desire to be shown into a room at once; and, as for Mrs. Squails, if the poor old woman honours me with her custom, I will turn her out a gown that shall be the envy of Hadleigh.'

Dulce did not answer this, but the droop of her lip was piteous; it melted Phillis at once.

'Oh, do cheer up, you silly girl!' she said, with a coaxing face. 'What is the good of making ourselves more miserable than we need? If you prefer the two little rooms with mother, say so; and Nan and I will look out for old ladies at once.'

'No! no! Oh, pray, don't leave me!' still more piteously.

'Well, what will you have us do? We cannot starve; and we don't mean to beg. Pluck up a little spirit, Dulce; see how good Nan is! You have no idea how comfortable we should be!' she went on, with judicious word-painting. 'We should all be together— that is the great thing. Then we could talk over our work; and in the afternoon, when we felt dreary, mother could read some interesting novel to us,'—a tremulous sigh from Nan at this point.

What a contrast to the afternoons at Glen Cottage—tennis, and five o'clock tea, and the company of their young friends! Phillis understood the sigh, and hurried on.

'It will not be always work. We will have long country walks in the evening; and then there will be the garden, and the seashore. Of course we must have exercise and recreation. I am afraid we shall have to do without society, for no one will visit ladies under such circumstances; but I would rather do without people than without each other, and so would Nan.'

'Yes, indeed!' broke in Nan; and now the tears were in her eyes.

Dulce grew suddenly ashamed of herself. She got up in a little flurry, and kissed them both.

'I was very naughty; but I did not mean to be unkind. I would rather carry parcels, and stand in halls—yes, and even make gowns for Mrs. Squails—than lose you both. I will be good. I will not worry you any more, Phil, with my nonsense; and I will work—you will see how I will work,' finished Dulce breathlessly.

'There's a darling!' said Nan; and then she added in a tired voice, 'But it is two o'clock—and Dick is coming this morning to say good-bye; and I want to ask you both particularly not to say a word to him about this. Let him go away and enjoy himself, and think we are going on as usual; it would spoil his holiday; and there is always time enough for bad news,' went on Nan, with a little tremble of her lip.

'Dear Nan, we understand,' returned Phillis gently; 'and you are right, as you always are. And now to bed—to bed,' she continued, in a voice of enforced cheerfulness; and then they all kissed each other very quietly and solemnly, and crept up as noiselessly as possible to their rooms.

Phillis and Dulce shared the same room; but Nan had a little chamber to herself very near her mother's—a door connected the two rooms. Nan closed this carefully, when she had ascertained that Mrs. Challoner was still sleeping, and then sat down by the window, and looked out into the gray glimmering light that preceded the dawn.

Sleep! how could she sleep, with all these thoughts surging through her mind, and knowing that in a few hours Dick would come and say good-bye? and here Nan broke down, and had such a fit of crying as she had not had since her father died; nervous, uncontrollable tears, that it was useless to stem in her tired, overwrought state.

They exhausted her, and disposed her for sleep. She was so chilled and weary, that she was glad to lie down in bed at last and close her eyes; and she had scarcely done so before drowsiness crept over her, and she knew no more until she found the sunshine flooding her little room, and Dorothy standing by her bed, asking rather crossly why no one seemed disposed to wake this beautiful morning.

'Am I late? oh, I hope I am not late!' exclaimed Nan, springing up in a moment. She dressed herself in quite a flurry, for fear she should keep anyone waiting. It was only at the last moment she remembered the outburst of the previous night, and wondered with some dismay what Dick would think of her pale cheeks, and the reddened lines round her eyes, and only hoped that he would not attribute them to his going away. Nan was only just in time, for as she entered the breakfast-room Dick came through the veranda, and put in his head at the window.

'Not at breakfast yet! and where are the others?' he asked, in some surprise, for the Challoners were early people, and very regular in their habits.

'We sat up rather late last night talking,' returned Nan, giving him her hand without looking at him, and yet Dick showed to advantage this morning in his new tweed travelling-suit.

'Well, I have only got ten minutes. I managed to give the pater the slip; he will be coming after me, I believe, if I stay longer. This is first-rate, having you all to myself this last morning. But what's up, Nan? you don't seem quite up to the mark. You are palish, you know, and——' here Dick paused in pained embarrassment. Were those traces of tears? had Nan really been crying? was she sorry about his going away? And now there was an odd lump in Dick's throat.

Nan understood the pause, and got frightened.

'It is nothing. I have a slight headache; there was a little domestic worry that wanted putting to rights,' stammered Nan; 'it worried me, for I am stupid at such things, you know.'

She was explaining herself somewhat lamely, and to no purpose, for Dick did not believe her in the least. 'Domestic worry!' as though she cared for such rubbish as that; as though any amount could make her cry—her, his bright high-spirited Nan! No; she had been fretting about their long separation, and his father's unkindness, and the difficulties ahead of them.

'I want you to give me a rose,' he said suddenly, *à propos* of nothing, as it seemed; but looking up, Nan caught a wistful gleam in his eyes, and hesitated. Was it not Dick who had told her that anecdote about the Queen, or was it Lothair? and did not a certain meaning attach to this gift? Dick was for ever picking roses for her; but he had never given her one, except with that meaning look on his face.

'You are hesitating,' he said, reproachfully; 'and on my last morning, when we shall not see each other for months.' And Nan moved towards the veranda slowly, and gathered a crimson one without a word, and put it in his hand.

'Thank you,' he said quite quietly; but he detained the hand as well as the rose for a moment. 'One day I will show you this again, and tell you what it means if you do not know; and then we shall see, ah, Nan, my——' He paused as Phillis's step entered the room, and said hurriedly, in a low voice, 'Good-bye; I will not go in again. I don't want to see any of them, only you—only you. Good-bye; take care of yourself for my sake, Nan!' and Dick looked at her wistfully, and dropped her hand.

'Has he gone?' asked Phillis, looking up in surprise as her sister came through the open window; 'has he gone without finding anything out?'

'Yes, he has gone, and he does not know anything,' replied Nan in a subdued voice, as she seated herself behind the urn. It was over now, and she was ready for anything.

‘ Take care of yourself for my sake, Nan !’—that was ringing in her ears; but she had not said a word in reply. Only the rose lay in his hand—her parting gift, and perhaps her parting pledge.

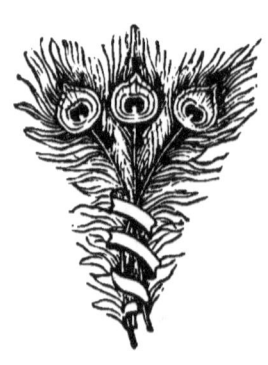

## CHAPTER IX.

### A LONG DAY.

NAN never recalled the memory of that 'long gray day,' as she inwardly termed it, without a shiver of discomfort.

Never but once in her bright young life had she known such a day, and that was when her dead father lay in the darkened house, and her widowed mother had crept weeping into her arms as to her only remaining refuge; but that stretched so far back into the past that it had grown into a vague remembrance.

It was not only that Dick was gone, though the pain of that separation was far greater than she would have believed possible, but a moral earthquake had shattered their little world, involving them in utter chaos.

It was only yesterday that she was singing ballads in the Longmead drawing-room—only yesterday; but to-day everything was changed. The sun shone, the birds sang, everyone ate and drank and moved about as usual. Nan talked and smiled, and no stranger would have guessed that much was amiss; nevertheless, a weight lay heavy on her spirits, and Nan knew in her secret heart that she could never be again the same light-hearted, easy-going creature that she was yesterday.

Later on, the sisters confessed to each other that the day had been perfectly interminable; the hours dragged on slowly, the sun seemed as though it never meant to set; to add to their trouble, their mother looked so ill when she came downstairs, wrapped in her soft white shawl in spite of the heat, that Nan thought of sending for a doctor, and only refrained at the remembrance that they had no right to such luxuries now except in cases of necessity.

Then Dorothy was in one of her impractic-

# A Long Day. 153

able moods, throwing cold water on all her young mistress's suggestions, and doing her best to disarrange the domestic machinery. Dorothy suspected a mystery somewhere; her young ladies had sat up half the night, and looked pale and owlish in the morning. If they chose to keep her in the dark, and not take her into their confidence, it was their affair; but she meant to show them what she thought of their conduct. So she contradicted and snapped, until Nan told her wearily that she was a disagreeable old thing, and left her and Susan to do as they liked. She knew Mr. Trinder was waiting for her in the dining-room, and as Mrs. Challoner was not well enough to see him, she and Phillis must entertain him.

He had slept at a friend's house a few miles from Oldfield, and was to lunch at Glen Cottage, and take the afternoon train to London.

He was not sorry when he heard Mrs. Challoner was too indisposed to receive him. In spite of his polite expressions of regret, he had found the poor lady terribly trying on the previous evening. She was a bad manager and had muddled her affairs, and she did not seem to understand half he told her; and her tears and lamentations when she had realized the truth had been too much for the soft-hearted old bachelor, though people did call him a woman-hater.

'But I never could bear to see a woman cry; it is as bad as watching an animal in pain,' he half-growled, as he drew out his red pocket-handkerchief and used it rather noisily.

It was easier work to explain everything to these two bright, sensible girls. Phillis listened and asked judicious questions; but Nan sat with downcast face, plaiting the table-cloth between her restless fingers, and thinking of Dick at odd intervals.

She took it all in, however, and roused up in earnest when Mr. Trinder had finished his explanations, and Phillis began to talk in her turn; she was actually taking the old lawyer into her confidence, and detailing their scheme in the most business-like way.

'The mother does not know yet—this is all in confidence; but Nan and I have made up our minds to take this step,' finished the young philosopher calmly.

'Bless my soul!' ejaculated Mr. Trinder—he had given vent to this expression at various intervals, but had not further interrupted her. 'Bless my soul! my dear young ladies, I think—excuse me if I am too abrupt, but you must be dreaming.'

Phillis shook her head smilingly; and as Dorothy came into the room that moment to lay the luncheon, she proposed a turn in the garden, and fetched Mr. Trinder's hat herself, and guided him to a side-walk, where they could not be seen from the drawing-room windows. Nan followed them, and tried to keep step with Mr. Trinder's shambling footsteps, as he walked between the girls with a hot perplexed face, and still muttering to himself at intervals.

'It is all in confidence,' repeated Phillis, in the same calm voice.

'And you are actually serious—you are not joking?'

'Do your clients generally joke when they are ruined?' returned Phillis, with natural exasperation. 'Do you think Nan and I are in such excellent spirits that we could originate such a piece of drollery? Excuse me, Mr. Trinder, but I must say I do not think your remark quite well timed;' and Phillis turned away with a little dignity.

'No, no! now you are put out, and no wonder!' returned Mr. Trinder soothingly; and he stood quite still on the gravel path, and fixed his keen little eyes on the two young creatures before him—Nan with her pale cheeks and sad eyes, and Phillis, alert, irritated, full of repressed energy. 'Dear, dear! what a pity!' groaned the old man; 'two such bonnie lasses! and to think a little management and listening to my advice would have kept the house over your heads! if only your mother would have hearkened to me!'

'It is too late for all that now, Mr. Trinder,' replied Phillis impatiently; 'isn't it waste of time crying over spilt milk when we must be taking our other goods to market? We must make the best of our poor little commodities,' sighed the girl. 'If we were only clever and accomplished we might do better; but now——' and Phillis left her sentence unfinished, which was a way she had, and which people thought very telling.

'But, my dear young lady, with all your

advantages, and——' here Phillis interrupted him rather brusquely.

'What advantages? do you mean we had a governess? Well, we had three, one after the other; and they were none of them likely to turn out first-rate pupils. Oh, we are well enough compared to other girls! if we had not to earn our own living, we should not be so much amiss. But, Nan, why don't you speak? why do you leave me all the hard work? Did you not tell us last night that you were not fit for a governess?'

Nan felt rather ashamed of her silence after this. It was true that she was leaving all the onus of their plan on Phillis, and it was certainly time for her to come to her rescue. So she quietly but rather shyly endorsed her sister's speech, and assured Mr. Trinder that they had carefully considered the matter from every point of view; and though it was a very poor prospect, and involved a great deal of work and self-sacrifice, she, Nan, thought that Phillis was right, and that it was the best, indeed the only thing they could do under the circumstances.

'For myself, I prefer it infinitely to letting

lodgings,' finished Nan; and Phillis looked at her gratefully.

But Mr. Trinder was obstinate, and had old-fashioned views, and argued the whole thing in his dictatorial masculine way. They sat down to luncheon and presently sent Dorothy away— a piece of independence that bitterly offended that crabbed but faithful individual — and wrangled busily through the whole of the meal.

Mr. Trinder never could remember afterwards whether it was lamb or mutton he had eaten; he had a vague idea that Dulce had handed him the mint-sauce, and that he had declined it and helped himself to salad. The doubt disturbed him for the first twenty miles of his homeward journey. 'Good gracious, for a man not to know whether he is eating lamb or mutton!' he soliloquized, as he vainly tried to enjoy his usual nap; 'but then I never was so upset in my life. Those pretty creatures, and Challoners too—bless my soul!' and here the lawyer's cogitations became confused and misty.

Nan, who had more than once seen tears in the lawyer's shrewd little gray eyes, had been very gentle and tolerant over the

## A Long Day. 159

old man's irritability; but Phillis had resented his caustic speeches somewhat hotly. Dulce, who was on her best behaviour, was determined not to interfere or say a word to thwart her sisters; she even went so far as to explain to Mr. Trinder that they would not have to carry parcels, as Phillis meant to hire a boy. She had no idea that this magnanimous speech was in a figurative manner the last straw that broke the camel's back. Mr. Trinder pushed back his chair hastily, made some excuse that his train must be due, and beat a retreat an hour before the time, unable to pursue such a painful subject any longer.

Nan rose with a sigh of relief, as soon as the door closed upon their visitor, and took refuge in the shady drawing-room with her mother, whom she found in a very tearful, querulous state, requiring a great deal of soothing. They had decided that no visitors were to be admitted that afternoon.

'You may say your mistress is indisposed with a bad headache, Dorothy, and that we are keeping the house quiet,' Nan remarked with a little dignity, with the remembrance of that late passage of arms.

'Very well, Miss Nan,' returned the old servant. However, she was a little cowed by Nan's manner; such an order had never before been given in the cottage. Mrs. Challoner's headaches were common events in everyday life, and had never been known before to interfere with their afternoon receptions. A little eau de Cologne and extra petting—a stronger cup of tea served up to her in her bedroom, had been the only remedies; the girls had always had their tennis as usual, and the sound of their voices and laughter had been as music in their mother's ears.

'Very well, Miss Nan,' was all Dorothy ventured to answer; but she withdrew with a face puckered up with anxiety. She took in the tea-tray unbidden at an earlier hour than usual; there were Dulce's favourite hot cakes, and some rounds of delicately buttered toast, 'for the young ladies have not eaten above a morsel at luncheon,' said Dorothy in explanation to her mistress.

'Never mind us,' returned Nan, with a friendly nod at the old woman; 'it has been so hot to-day.' And then she coaxed her mother to eat, and made believe herself to enjoy the repast; and the sweet cake crumbled in her fingers, as she wondered how many more evenings they would spend in the pretty drawing-room on which they had expended so much labour.

Nan had countermanded the late dinner, which they all felt would be a pretence and mockery; and as Mrs. Challoner's headache refused to yield to the usual remedies, she was obliged to retire to bed as soon as the sun set, and the three girls went out in the garden, and walked up and down the lawn with their arms interlaced, while Dorothy watched them from the pantry window, and wiped away a tear or two, as she washed up the tea-things.

'How I should like a long walk!' exclaimed Dulce impatiently. 'It is so narrow and confined here; but it would never do—we should meet people.'

'No, it would never do,' agreed her sisters, feeling a fresh pang that such avoidance was necessary. They had never hidden anything before, and the thought that this mystery lay between them and their friends was exquisitely painful.

'I feel as though I never cared to see one of them again!' sighed poor Nan, for which speech she was rather sharply rebuked by Phillis.

They settled a fair amount of business before they went to bed that night; and when Dorothy brought in the supper-tray, bearing a little covered dish in triumph, which she set down before Nan, Nan looked at her with grave, reproachful eyes, in which there was a great deal of kindness.

'You should not do this, Dorothy,' she said very gently; 'we cannot afford such delicacies now.'

'It is your favourite dish, Miss Nan,' returned Dorothy, quite ignoring this remark. 'Susan has cooked it to a nicety; but it will be spoiled if it is not eaten hot.' And she stood over them while Nan dispensed the dainty. 'You must eat it while it is hot,' she kept saying as she fidgeted about the room, taking up things and putting them down again. Phillis looked at Nan with a comical expression of dismay.

'Dorothy, come here,' she exclaimed at last, pushing away her plate. 'Don't you see that Susan is wasting all her talents on us, and that we can't eat to-day?'

'Everyone can eat if they try, Miss Phillis,' replied Dorothy oracularly. 'But a thing like that must be hot, or it is spoiled.'

'Oh, never mind about it being hot,' returned Phillis, beginning to laugh. She was so tired, and Dorothy was such a droll old thing; and how were even stewed pigeons to be appetizing under the circumstances?

'Oh, you may laugh,' began Dorothy, in an offended tone; but Phillis took hold of her and nearly shook her.

'Oh, what a stupid old thing you are! Don't you know what a silly, aggravating old creature you can be when you like? If I laugh, it is because everything is so ludicrous and wretched. Nan and Dulce are not laughing.'

'No, indeed,' put in Dulce; 'we are far, far too unhappy!'

'What is it, Miss Nan?' asked Dorothy, sidling up to her in a coaxing manner. 'I am only an old servant, but it was me that put Miss Dulce in her father's arms—"the pretty lamb," as he called her; and she with a skin like a lily. If there is trouble, you would not keep it from her old nurse, surely?'

'No, indeed, Dorothy; we want to tell you,' returned Nan, touched by this appeal; and then she quietly recapitulated the main points that concerned their difficulties—their mother's loss, their future poverty, the necessity for leaving Glen Cottage and settling down at the Friary.

'We shall all have to work,' finished Nan, with prudent vagueness, not daring to entrust their plan to Dorothy; 'the cottage is small, and, of course, we can only keep one servant.'

'I dare say I shall be able to manage if you will help me a little,' returned Dorothy, drying her old eyes with the corner of her apron. 'Dear, dear! to think of such an affliction coming upon my mistress and the dear young ladies! It is like an earthquake or a flood, or something sudden and unexpected—Lord deliver us! And to think of my speaking crossly to you, Miss Nan, and you with all this worry on your mind!'

'We will not think of that,' returned Nan soothingly. 'Susan's quarter will be up shortly, and we must get her away as soon

## A Long Day. 165

as possible. My great fear is that the work may be too much for you, poor Dorothy; and that—that—we may have to keep you waiting sometimes for your wages,' she added, rather hesitatingly, fearing to offend Dorothy's touchy temper, and yet determined to put the whole matter clearly before her.

'I don't think we need talk about that,' returned Dorothy, with dignity. 'I have not saved up my wages for nineteen years without having a nest-egg laid up for rainy days. Wages—when I mention the word, Miss Nan,' went on Dorothy, waxing somewhat irate, 'it will be time enough to enter upon that subject. I haven't deserved such a speech; no, that I haven't,' went on Dorothy, with a sob. 'Wages indeed!'

'Now, nursey, you shan't be cross with Nan,' cried Dulce, throwing her arms round the old woman; for in spite of her eighteen years she was still Dorothy's special charge. 'She's quite right; it may be an unpleasant subject, but we will not have you working for us for nothing.'

'Very well, Miss Dulce,' returned Dorothy, in a choked voice, preparing to withdraw;

but Nan caught hold of the hard work-worn hand, and held her fast.

'Oh, Dorothy, you would not add to our trouble now, when we are so terribly unhappy! I never meant to hurt your feelings by what I said. If you will only go to the Friary and help us to make the dear mother comfortable, I, for one, will be deeply grateful.'

'And you will not talk of wages?' asked Dorothy, mollified by Nan's sweet, pleading tones.

'Not until we can afford to do so,' returned Nan hastily, feeling that this was a safe compromise, and that they should be eked out somehow. And then, the stewed pigeons being regarded as a failure, Dorothy consented to remove the supper-tray, and the long day was declared at an end.

## CHAPTER X.

#### THE FRIARY.

LDFIELD was rather mystified by the Challoners' movements. There were absolutely three afternoons during which Nan and her sisters were invisible. There was a tennis-party at the Paines' on one of these days, but at the last minute they had excused themselves. Nan's prettily worded note was declared very vague and unsatisfactory, and on the following afternoon there was a regular invasion of the cottage: Carrie Paine, and two of the Twentyman girls, and Adelaide Sartoris, and her young brother Albert.

They found Dulce alone, looking very sad and forlorn.

'Nan and Phillis had gone down to Hadleigh that morning,' she explained, in rather a confused way; 'they were not expected back until the following evening.'

On being pressed by Miss Sartoris as to the reason of this sudden trip, she added, rather awkwardly, that it was on business—her mother was not well—oh, very far from well; and they had to look at a house that belonged to them, as the tenant had lately died.

This was all very plausible; but Dulce's manner was so constrained, and she spoke with such hesitation, that Miss Sartoris was convinced that something lay behind. They went out in the garden, however, and chose sides for their game of tennis; and though Dulce had never played so badly in her life, the fresh air and exercise did her good, and at the end of the afternoon she looked a little less drooping.

It was felt to be a failure, however, by the whole party; and when tea was over, there was no mention of a second game. 'No, we will not stay any longer,' observed Isabella Twentyman, kissing the girl with much affection. 'Of course we understand that you will be wanting to sit with your mother.

'Yes, and if you do not come in to-morrow we shall quite know how it is,' added Miss Sartoris good-naturedly, for which Dulce thanked her and looked relieved.

She stood at the hall-door watching them as they walked down the village swinging their rackets and talking merrily.

'What happy girls!' she thought, with a sigh. Miss Sartoris was an heiress, and the Twentymans were rich, and everyone knew that Carrie and Sophy Paine would have money. 'None of them will have to work,' said poor Dulce sorrowfully to herself; 'they can go on playing tennis and driving and riding and dancing as long as they like;' and then she went up to her mother's room with lagging footsteps and a cloudy brow.

'You may depend upon it there is something amiss with those Challoners,' said Miss Sartoris, as soon as they were out of sight of the cottage; 'no one has seen anything of them for the last three or four days, and I never saw Dulce so unlike herself.'

'Oh, I hope not,' returned Carrie gravely, who had heard enough from her father to guess that there was pecuniary embarrassment at the bottom. 'Poor little thing, she did seem rather subdued. How many people do you expect to muster to-morrow, Adelaide?' and then Miss Sartoris understood that the subject was to be changed.

While Dulce was trying to entertain her friends, Nan and Phillis were reconnoitring the Friary.

They had taken an early train to London, and had contrived to reach Hadleigh a little before three. They went first to Beach House—a small unpretending house on the Parade kept by a certain Mrs. Mózley, with whom they had once lodged after Dulce had had the measles.

The good woman received them with the utmost cordiality. Her place was pretty nearly filled, she told them proudly; the drawing-room had been taken for three months, and an elderly couple were in the dining-room.

'But there is a bedroom I could let you have for one night,' finished Mrs. Mozley, 'and there is the little side parlour where you could have your tea and breakfast.' And when Nan had thanked her, and suggested the addition of chops to their evening meal, they left their modest luggage and set out for the Friary.

Phillis would have gone direct to their destination, but Nan pleaded for one turn on the Parade. She wanted a glimpse of the sea, and it was such a beautiful afternoon.

The tide was out, and the long black breakwaters were uncovered; the sun was shining on the wet shingles and narrow strip of yellow sand. The sea looked blue and unruffled, with little sparkles and gleams of light, and white sails glimmered on the horizon. Some boatmen were dragging a boat down the beach; it grated noisily over the pebbles. A merry party were about to embark—a tall man in a straw hat and two boys in knickerbockers. Their sisters were watching them. 'Oh, Reggie, do be careful!' Nan heard one of the girls say, as he waded knee-deep into the water.

'Come, Nan, we ought not to dawdle like this!' exclaimed Phillis impatiently; and they went on quickly—past the long row of old-fashioned white houses with the green before them, and that sweet Sussex border of soft feathery tamarisk; and then past the cricketfield, and down to the whitewashed cottages of the Preventive Station; and then they turned back and walked towards the Steyne, and after that Nan declared herself satisfied.

There were plenty of people on the Parade, and most of them looked after the two girls as they passed. Nan's sweet bloom and graceful carriage always attracted notice; and Phillis, although she generally suffered from comparison with her sister, was still very uncommon-looking.

'I should like to know who those young ladies are,' observed a military-looking man with a white moustache, who was standing at the library-door waiting for his daughter to make some purchases. 'Look at them, Elizabeth: one of them is such a pretty girl, and they walk so well.'

'Dear father, I suppose they are only some new-comers; we shall see their names down in the visitors' list by-and-by;' and Miss Middleton smiled as she took her father's arm, for she was slightly lame. She knew strangers always interested him, and that he would make it his business for the next few days to find out everything about them.

'Did you see that nice-looking woman?' asked Phillis, when they had passed. 'She was quite young, only her hair was grey—fancy, a grey-haired girl!'

'Oh, she must be older than she looks,' returned Nan indifferently.

She was not looking at people; she was far too busily engaged identifying each well-remembered spot.

There was the shabby little cottage where she and her mother had once stayed after an illness of Mrs. Challoner's. What odd little rooms they had occupied, looking over a strip of garden-ground full of marigolds! 'Marigolds-all-in-a-row Cottage' she had named it in her home letters. It was nearly opposite the White House where Mrs. Cheyne lived. Nan remembered her, a handsome sad-looking woman, who always wore black, and drove out in such handsome carriages.

'Always alone—how sad!' Nan thought; and she wondered, as they walked past the low stone walls with grassy mounds sloping from them, and a belt of shrubbery shutting out views of the house, whether Mrs. Cheyne lived there still.

They had reached a quiet country corner now; there was a clump of trees, guarded by posts and chains; a white house stood far back. There were two or three other houses, and a cottage dotted down here and there. The road looked shady and inviting. Nan began to look about her more cheerfully.

'I am glad it is so quiet, and so far away from the town, and that our neighbours will not be able to overlook us.'

'I was just thinking of that as a disadvantage,' returned Phillis, with placid opposition. 'It is a pity, under the circumstances, that we are not nearer the town;' and after that Nan held her peace.

They were passing an old-fashioned house with a green door in the wall, when it suddenly opened, and a tall, grave-looking young man, in clerical attire, came out quickly upon them, and then drew back to let them pass.

'I suppose that is the new vicar?' whispered Phillis, when they had gone a few steps. 'You know poor old Dr. Musgrave is dead, and most likely that is his successor.'

'I forgot that was the Vicarage,' returned

## The Friary. 175

Nan. But happily she did not turn round to look at it again; if she had done so, she would have seen the young clergyman still standing by the green door watching them. 'It is a shabby, dull old house in front; but I remember when mother and I returned Mrs. Musgrave's call, that we were shown into such a dear old-fashioned drawing-room, with windows looking out on such a pleasant garden. I quite fell in love with it.'

'Well, we shall be near neighbours,' observed Phillis somewhat shortly, as she paused before another green door, set in a long blank wall; 'for here we are at the Friary, and I had better just run over the way, and get the key from Mrs. Crump.'

Nan nodded, and then stood like an image of patience before the shabby green door. Would it open and let them into a new untried life? What sort of fading hopes, of dim regrets, would be left outside when they crossed the threshold? The thought of the empty rooms, not yet swept and garnished, made her shiver; the upper windows looked blankly at her, like blind, unrecognising eyes. She was quite glad when Phillis joined her again, swinging the key on her little finger, and humming a tune in forced cheerfulness.

'What a dull, shut-in place! I think the name of Friary suits it exactly,' observed Nan disconsolately, as they went up the little flagged path, bordered with lilac bushes. 'It feels like a miniature convent or prison; we might have a grating in the door, and answer all outsiders through it.'

'Nonsense!' returned Phillis, who was determined to take a bright view of things. 'Don't go into the house just yet; I want to see the garden;' and she led the way down a gloomy side-path, with unclipped box and yews, that made it dark and decidedly damp. This brought them to a little lawn, with tall, rank grass that might have been mown for hay, and some side-beds full of old-fashioned flowers, such as lupins and monkshood, pinks and small pansies; a dreary little greenhouse, with a few empty flower-pots and a turned-up box, was in one corner, and an attempt at a rockery, with a periwinkle climbing over it, and an undesirable number of oyster-shells.

An old medlar-tree, very warped and

gnarled, was at the bottom of the lawn, and beyond this a small kitchen-garden, with abundance of gooseberry and currant bushes, and vast resources in shape of mint, marjoram, and lavender.

'Oh dear, oh dear! what a wretched little place after our dear old Glen Cottage garden!' and in spite of her good resolutions Nan's eyes grew misty.

'Comparisons are odious,' retorted Phillis briskly. 'We have just to make the best of things—and I don't deny they are horrid—and put all the rest away, between lavender, on the shelves of our memory;' and she smiled grimly as she picked one of the grey spiky flowers.

And then as they walked round the weedy paths, she pointed out how different it would look when the lawn was mown, and all the weeds and oyster-shells removed, and the box and yews clipped, and a little paint put on the green-house.

'And look at that splendid passion-flower, growing like a weed over the back of the cottage,' she remarked with a wave of her hand; 'it only wants training and nailing up.

Poor Miss Monks has neglected the garden shamefully; but then she was always ailing.'

They went into the cottage after this. The entry was rather small and dark. The kitchen came first; it was of a tolerable size apartment, with two windows looking out on the lilacs, and the green door, and the blank wall.

'I am afraid Dorothy will find it a little dull,' Nan observed rather ruefully. And again she thought the name of Friary was well given to this gruesome cottage; but she cheered up when Phillis opened cupboards and showed her a light little scullery, and thought that perhaps they could make it comfortable for Dorothy.

The other two rooms looked upon the garden; one had three windows, and was really a very pleasant parlour.

'This must be our work-room,' began Phillis solemnly, as she stood in the centre of the empty room, looking round her with bright knowing glances. 'Oh, what an ugly paper, Nan! but we can easily put up a prettier one. The smaller room must be where we live and take our meals; it is not quite so cheerful as this. It is so nice having this side window; it will give us more light, and we shall be able to see who comes in at the door.'

'Yes, that is an advantage,' assented Nan. She was agreeably surprised to find such a good-sized room in the cottage; it was decidedly low, and the windows were not plate-glass, but she thought that on summer mornings they might sit there very comfortably looking out at the lawn and the medlar-tree.

'We shall be glad of these cupboards,' she suggested, after a pause, while Phillis took out sundry pieces of tape from her pocket, and commenced making measurements in a business-like manner. 'Our work will make such a litter, and I should like things to be as tidy as possible. I am thinking,' she continued, 'we might have mother's great carved wardrobe in the recess behind the door. It is really a magnificent piece of furniture, and in a work-room it would not be so out of place; we could hang up the finished and unfinished dresses in it out of the dust. And we could have the little drawing-room chiffonnier between the windows for our pieces, and odds and ends in the cupboards. It is a pity our table is round; but perhaps it will look all the more comfortable. The sewing-machine must be in the side window,' added Nan, who was quite in her element now, for she loved all housewifely arrangements; 'and mother's easy-chair and little table must stand by the fireplace. My davenport will be useful for papers and accounts.'

'It is really a very convenient room,' returned Phillis in a satisfied voice, when they had exhausted its capabilities; and though the second parlour was small and dull in comparison, even Nan dropped no disparaging word.

Both of them agreed it would do very well. There was a place for the large roomy couch that their mother so much affected, and their favourite chairs and knick-knacks would soon make it look cosy; and after this they went upstairs hand in hand.

There were only four bedrooms, and two of these were not large; the most cheerful one was of course allotted to their mother, and the next in size must be for Phillis and

Dulce. Nan was to have a small one next to her mother.

The evening was drawing on by the time they had finished their measurements and left the cottage. Nan, who was tired and wanted her tea, was for hurrying on to Beach House; but Phillis insisted on calling at the Library. She wanted to put some inquiries to Miss Milner. To-morrow they would have the paper-hanger, and look out for a gardener, and there was Mrs. Crump to interview about cleaning down the cottage.

'Oh. very well,' returned Nan wearily, and she followed Phillis into the shop, where good-natured bustling Miss Milner came to them at once.

Phillis put the question to her in a low voice, for there were other customers exchanging books over the counter. The same young clergyman they had before noticed had just bought a local paper, and was waiting evidently for a young lady who was turning over some magazines quite close to them.

'Do we know of a good dressmaker in the place?' repeated Miss Milner in her loud cheerful voice, very much to Nan's discomfort, for the clergyman looked up from his paper at once. 'Miss Monks was a tolerable fit—but, poor thing! she died a few weeks ago; and Mrs. Slasher, who lives over Viner's the haberdasher's, cannot hold a candle to her. Miss Masham, there'—pointing to a smart ringleted young person, evidently her assistant—'had her gown ruined by her—hadn't you, Miss Masham?'

Miss Masham simpered, but her reply was inaudible; but the young lady who was standing near them suddenly turned round.

'There is Mrs. Langley, who lives just by. I shall be very happy to give these ladies her address, for she is a widow with little children, and I am anxious to procure her work——' and then she looked at Nan, and hesitated; 'that is, if you are not very particular,' she added with sudden embarrassment, for even in her morning dress there was a certain style about Nan that distinguished her from other people.

'Thank you, Miss Drummond,' returned Miss Milner gratefully. 'Shall I write down the address for you, ma'am?'

'Yes—no—thank you very much, but

perhaps it does not matter,' returned Nan hurriedly, feeling awkward for the first time in her life. But Phillis, who realized all the humour of the situation, interposed.

'The address will do us no harm, and we may as well have it, although we should not trouble Mrs. Langley. I will call in again, Miss Milner, to-morrow morning, and then I will explain what it is we really want. We are in a hurry now,' continued Phillis loftily, turning away with a dignified inclination of her head towards the officious stranger.

Phillis was not prepossessed in her favour. She was a dark, wiry little person—not exactly plain, but with an odd, comical face; and she was dressed so dowdily and with such utter disregard of taste, that Phillis instinctively felt Mrs. Langley was not to be dreaded.

'What a queer little body! Do you think she belongs to him?' she asked Nan, as they walked rapidly towards Beach House.

'What in the world made you strike in after that fashion?' demanded the young man, as he and his companion followed more slowly in the strangers' footsteps; 'that is just your way, Mattie, interfering and meddling in other folks' affairs. Why cannot you mind your own business sometimes,' he continued irritably, 'instead of putting your foot into other people's?'

'You are as cross as two sticks this afternoon, Archie,' returned his sister composedly. She had a sharp little pecking voice that seemed to match her, somehow; for she was not unlike a bright-eyed bird, and had quick pouncing movements. 'Wait a moment; my braid has got torn, and is dragging.'

'I wish you would think a little more of my position, and take greater pains with your appearance,' returned her brother, in an annoyed voice. 'What would Grace say to see what a fright you make of yourself! It is a sin and a shame for a woman to be untidy or careless in her dress—it is unfeminine—it is unladylike!' hurling each separate epithet at her.

Perhaps Miss Drummond was used to these compliments, for she merely pinned her braid without seeming the least put out.

'I think I am a little shabby,' she remarked tranquilly, as they at last walked on. 'Perhaps Mrs. Langley had better make me a dress too,' with a laugh, for in spite of her sharp voice, she was an even-tempered little body; but this last remark only added fuel to his wrath.

'You really have less sense than a child. The idea of recommending a person like Mrs. Langley to those young ladies—a woman who works for Miss Masham!'

'They were very plainly dressed, Archie,' returned poor Mattie, who felt this last snub acutely; for if there was one thing upon which she prided herself, it was her good sense. 'They had dark print dresses—not as good as the one I have on—and nothing could be quieter.'

'Oh, you absurd little goose!' exclaimed her brother, and he burst into a laugh, for the drollery of the comparison restored him to instant good-humour. 'If you cannot see the difference between that frumpish gown of yours, with its little bobtails and fringes, and those pretty dresses before us, I must say you are as blind as a bat, Mattie.'

'Oh, never mind my gown!' returned Mattie, with a sigh.

She had had these home-thrusts to meet

and parry nearly every day, ever since she had come to keep house for this fastidious brother. She was a very active, bustling little person, who had done a great deal of tough work in her day; but she never could be made to see that unless a woman add the graces of life to the cardinal virtues, she is comparatively speaking a failure in the eyes of the other sex.

So though Mattie was a frugal housekeeper, and worked from morning to night in his service—the veriest little drudge that was ever seen—she was a perpetual eyesore to her brother, who loved feminine grace and repose —whose tastes were fastidious and somewhat arbitrary. And so it was poor Mattie had more censure than praise, and wrote home piteous letters complaining that nothing she did seemed to satisfy Archie; and that her mother had made a great mistake in sending her, and not Grace, to preside over his bachelor establishment.

'Oh, Phillis, how shall we have courage to publish our plan!' exclaimed Nan, when they were at last discussing the much-needed tea and chops in the little parlour at Beach House.

The window was wide open. The returning tide was coming in with a pleasant ripple and wash over the shingle. The Parade was nearly empty; but some children's voices sounded from the green space before the houses. The brown sail of a fishing craft dipped into the horizon. It was so cool, so quiet, so restful; but Nan's eyes were weary, and she put the question wistfully.

Phillis looked into the teapot to gain a moment's reprieve; the corners of her mouth had an odd pucker in them.

'I never said it was not hard,' she burst out at last. 'I felt like a fool myself while I was speaking to Miss Milner; but then that clergyman was peeping at us between the folds of his paper. He seemed a nice-looking gentlemanly sort of man. Do you think that queer little lady in the plaid dress could be his wife? Oh no; I remember Miss Milner addressed her as Miss Drummond. Then she must be his sister—how odd!'

'Why should it be odd?' remarked Nan absently, who had not particularly noticed them..

'Oh, she was such a dowdy little thing,

not a bit nice-looking, and he was quite handsome, and looked rather distinguished. You know I always take stock of people, and make up my mind about them at once. And then we are to be such close neighbours.'

'I don't suppose we shall see much of them,' was Nan's somewhat depressed reply; and then, as they had finished their tea, they placed themselves at the open window, and began to talk about the business of next day; and, in discussing cupboards and new papers, Nan forgot her fatigue, and grew so interested that it was quite late before they thought of retiring to rest.

## CHAPTER XI.

'TELL US ALL ABOUT IT, NAN.'

NAN overslept herself, and was rather late the next morning; but as she entered the parlour, with an exclamation of penitence for her tardiness, she found her little speech was addressed to the empty walls. A moment after a shadow crossed the window, and Phillis came in.

She went up to Nan and kissed her, and there was a gleam of fun in her eyes.

'Oh, you lazy girl!' she said; 'leaving me all the hard work to do. Do you know, I have been round to the Library, and have had it all out with Miss Milner; and in the Steyne I met the clergyman again, and, would you believe it, he looked quite disappointed because you were not there!'

'Nonsense!' returned Nan sharply. She never liked these sort of joking speeches; they seemed treasonable to Dick.

'Oh, but he did,' persisted Phillis, who was a little excited and reckless after her morning's work. 'He threw me a disparaging glance, which said as plainly as possible, "Why are you not the other one?" That comes from having a sister handsomer than one's self.'

'Oh, Phillis! when people always think you so nice, and when you are so clever!'

Phillis got up and executed a little curtsey in the prettiest way, and then she sank down upon her chair in pretended exhaustion.

'What I have been through! But I have come out of it alive. Confess, now, there's a dear, that you could not have done it!'

'No, indeed,' with an alarmed air. 'Do you really mean to say that you actually told Miss Milner what we meant to do?'

'I told her everything. There, sit down and begin your breakfast, Nan, or we shall never be ready. I found her alone in the shop. Thank goodness, that Miss Masham was not there. I have taken a dislike to that simpering young person, and would rather make a dress for Mrs. Squails any day than for her. I told her the truth, without a bit of disguise. Would you believe it, the good creature actually cried about it! she quite upset me, too. "Such young ladies! dear, dear! one does not often see such," she kept saying over and over again. And then she put out her hand and stroked my dress, and said, "Such a beautiful fit, too; and to think you have made it yourself! such a clever young lady! Oh dear! what ever will Mr. Drummond and Miss Mattie say?" Stupid old thing! as though we cared what he said!'

'Oh, Phillis! and she cried over it?'

'She did indeed. I am not exaggerating. Two big round tears rolled down her cheeks. I could have kissed her for them. And then she made me sit down in the little room behind the shop, where she was having her breakfast, and poured me out a cup of tea, and——' But here Nan interrupted her, and there was a trace of anxiety in her manner.

'Poured you out a cup of tea! Miss Milner! And you drank it?'

'Of course I drank it; it was very good, and I was thirsty.'

But here Nan pounced upon her unexpectedly, and dragged her to the window.

'Your fun is only make-believe; there is no true ring about it. Let me see your eyes. Oh, Phil, Phil! I thought so! You have been crying, too!'

Phillis looked a little taken aback. Nan was too sharp for her. She tried to shake herself free a little pettishly.

'Well, if I choose to make a fool of myself for once in my life, you need not be silly about it; the old thing was so upsetting, and —and it was so hard to get it out.' Phillis would not have told for worlds how utterly she had broken down over that task of hers; how the stranger's sympathy had touched so painful a chord, that before she knew what she was doing, she had laid her head down on the counter, and was crying like a baby—all the more that she had so bravely pent up her feelings all these days that she might not dishearten her sisters.

But as Nan petted and praised her, she did tell how good Miss Milner had been to her.

'Fancy a fat old thing like that having such fine feelings,' she said, with an attempt to recover her sprightliness. 'She was as good as a mother to me; made me sit in the easy chair, and brought me some elder-flower water to bathe my eyes, and tried to cheer me up by saying that we should have plenty of work. She has promised not to tell anyone just yet about us; but when we are really in the Friary she will speak to people and recommend us, and—' here Phillis gave a little laugh—'we are to make up a new black silk for her that her brother has just sent her. Oh, dear, what will mother say to us, Nan?' And Phillis looked at her in an alarmed, beseeching way, as though in sore need of comfort.

Nan looked grave; but there was no hesitation in her answer.

'I am afraid it is too late to think of that now, Phil; it has to be done, and we must just go through with it.'

'You are right, Nanny darling, we must just go through it,' agreed Phillis; and then they went on with their unfinished breakfast, and after that the business of the day began.

It was late in the evening when they reached home. Dulce, who was at the gate looking out for them, nearly smothered them with kisses.

'Oh, you dear things! how glad I am to get you back!' she said, holding them both. 'Have you really only been away since yesterday morning? It seems a week, at least.'

'You ridiculous child; as though we believe that. But how is mother?'

'Oh, pretty well; but she will be better now you are back. Do you know,' eyeing them both very gravely, 'I think it was a wise thing of you to go away like that; it has shown me that mother and I could not do without you at all—we should have pined away in those lodgings; it has quite reconciled me to the plan,' finished Dulce, in a loud whisper that reached her mother's ears.

'What plan? What are you talking about, Dulce? and why do you keep your sisters standing in the hall?' asked Mrs. Challoner, a little irritably. But her brief nervousness vanished at the sight of their faces; she wanted nothing more, she told herself, but to see them round her, and hear their voices.

She grew quite cheerful when Phillis told her about the new papers, and how Mrs. Crump was to clean down the cottage; and how Crump had promised to mow the grass, and paint the greenhouse, and Jack and Bobbie were to weed the garden-paths.

'It is a perfect wilderness now, mother—you never saw such a place.'

'Never mind, so that it will hold us, and that we shall all be together,' she returned, with a smile. 'But Dulce talked of some plan—you must let me hear it, my dears; you must not keep me in the dark about anything. I know we shall all have to work,' continued the poor lady; 'but if we be all together, if you will promise not to leave me, I think I could bear anything.'

'Are we to tell her?' motioned Nan with her lips to Phillis; and as Phillis nodded 'Yes,' Nan gently and quietly began unfolding their plan.

But with all her care and all Phillis's promptings, the revelation was a great shock to Mrs. Challoner; in her weakened state she seemed hardly able to bear it.

Dulce repented bitterly of her incautious whisper when she saw her sisters' tired faces, and their fruitless attempts to soften the effects of such a blow. For a little while Mrs. Challoner seemed on the brink of despair; she would not listen; she abandoned herself to lamentations; she became so hysterical at last that Dorothy was summoned from the kitchen and taken into confidence.

'Mother, you are breaking our hearts,' Nan said, at last. She was kneeling at her feet, chafing her hands, and Phillis was fanning her; but she pushed them both away from her with weak violence.

'It is I whose heart is breaking! Why must I live to see such things? Dorothy, do you know my daughters are going to be dressmakers?—my daughters, who are Challoners—who have been delicately nurtured—who might hold up their heads with anyone?'

'Dorothy, hold your tongue!' exclaimed Phillis peremptorily. 'You are not to speak; this is for us to decide, and no one else. Mammy, you are making Nan look quite pale;

she is dreadfully tired, and so am I. Why
need we decide anything to-night? Everyone
is upset and excited, and when that is the
case one can never arrive at any proper conclusion. Let us talk about it to-morrow,
when we are rested;' and though Mrs. Challoner would not allow herself to be comforted,
Nan's fatigue and paleness were so visible to
her maternal eyes that they were more
eloquent than Phillis's words.

'I must not think only of myself. Yes,
yes. I will do as you wish. There will be
time enough for this sort of talk to-morrow.
Dorothy, will you help me? The young
ladies are tired; they have had a long journey.
No, my dear, no,' as Dulce pressed forward;
'I would rather have Dorothy,' and as the
old servant gave them a warning glance they
were obliged to let her have her way.

'Mammy has never been like this before,'
pouted Dulce, when they were left alone.
'She drives us away from her as though we
had done something purposely to vex her.'

'It is because she cannot bear the sight of
us to-night,' returned Phillis solemnly. 'It
is worse for her than for us; a mother feels

things for her children more than for herself;
it is nature, that is what it is,' she finished
philosophically; 'but she will be better to-
morrow,' and after this the miserable little
conclave broke up.

Mrs. Challoner passed a sleepless night,
and her pillow was sown with thorns. To
think of the Challoners falling so low as this!
'To think of her pretty Nan, her clever, bright
Phillis, her pet Dulce coming to this; oh, the
pity of it!' she cried, in the dark hours, when
vitality runs lowest, and thoughts seem to
flow involuntarily towards a dark centre.

But with the morning came sunshine, and
her girls' faces—a little graver than usual,
perhaps, but still full of youth and the brightness of energy; and the sluggish nightmare of
yesterday's grief began to fade a little.

'Now, mammy, you are not going to be
naughty to-day,' was Dulce's morning saluta-
tion as she seated herself on the bed.

Mrs. Challoner smiled faintly.

'Was I very naughty last night, Dulce?'

'Oh, as bad as possible. You pushed poor
Nan and Phillis away, and would not let anyone come near you but that cross old Dorothy,

and you never bade us good-night; but if you promise to be good, I will forgive you and make it up,' finished Dulce, with those light butterfly kisses to which she was addicted.

'Now, Chatterbox, it is my turn,' interrupted Phillis; and then she began a carefully concocted little speech, very cleverly drawn out to suit her mother's sensitive peculiarities.

She went over the old ground patiently point by point. Mrs. Challoner shuddered at the idea of letting lodgings.

'I knew you would agree with us,' returned Phillis, with a convincing nod; and then she went on to the next clause.

Mrs. Challoner argued a great deal about the governess scheme. She was quite angry with Phillis, and seemed to suffer a great deal of self-reproach when the girl spoke of their defective education and lack of accomplishments. Nan had to come to her sister's rescue; but the mother was slow to yield the point.

'I don't know what you mean. My girls are not different to other girls. What would your poor father say if he were alive? It is cruel to say this to me, when I stinted myself to give you every possible advantage—and I paid Miss Martin eighty pounds a year,' she concluded tearfully, feeling as though she were the victim of a fraud.

She was far more easily convinced that going out as companions would be impracticable under the circumstances. 'Oh no, that will never do!' she cried, when the two little rooms with Dulce were proposed; and after this Phillis found her task less difficult. She talked her mother over at last to reluctant acquiescence with her plan. 'I never knew how I came to consent,' she said afterwards, 'but they were too much for me.'

'We cannot starve. I suppose I must give in to you,' she said at last; 'but I shall never hold up my head again;' and she really believed what she said.

'Mother, you must trust us,' replied Phillis, touched by this victory she had won. ''Do you know what I said to Dulce? " Work cannot degrade us. Though we are dressmakers, we are still Challoners. Nothing can make us lose our dignity and self-respect as gentlewomen." '

'Other people will not recognise it,' returned her mother, with a sigh. 'You will lose caste. No one will visit you. Among your equals you will be treated as an inferior. It is this that bows me to the earth with shame.'

'Mother, how can you talk so!' cried Nan, in a clear indignant voice. 'What does it matter if people do not visit us? We must have a world of our own, and be sufficient for ourselves, if we can only keep together. Is not that what you have said to us over and over again? Well, we shall be together—we shall have each other. What does the outside world matter to us, after all?'

'Oh, you are young—you do not know what complications may arise,' replied Mrs. Challoner, with the gloomy forethought of middle age. She thought she knew the world better than they, but in reality she was almost as guileless and ignorant as her daughters. 'Until you begin, you do not know the difficulties that will beset you,' she went on.

But notwithstanding this foreboding speech, she was somewhat comforted by Nan's words—'they would be together!' Well, if Providence chose to inflict this humiliation and afflictive dispensation on her, it could be borne as long as she had her children around her.

Nan made one more speech—a somewhat stern one for her:

'Our trouble will be a furnace to try our friends. We shall know the true from the false. Only those who are really worth the name will be faithful to us.'

Nan was thinking of Dick; but her mother misunderstood her, and grew alarmed.

'You will not tell the Paines and the other people about here what you intend to do, surely? I could not bear that; no, indeed, I could not bear that!'

'Do not be afraid, dear mother,' returned Nan sadly; 'we are far too great cowards to do such a thing, and after all, there is no need to put ourselves to needless pain. If the Maynes were here we might not be able to keep it from them, perhaps, and so I am thankful they are away.'

Nan said this quite calmly, though her mother fixed her eyes upon her in a most tenderly mournful fashion. She had quite forgotten their Longmead neighbours, but now, as Nan recalled them to her mind, she remembered Mr. Mayne, and her look had become compassionate.

'It will be all over with those poor children,' she thought to herself; 'the father will never allow it—never—and I cannot wonder at him;' and then her heart softened to the memory of Dick, whom she had never thought good enough for Nan, for she remembered now with a sore pang that her pride was laid low in the dust, and that she could not hope now that her daughters would make splendid matches; even Dick would be above them, though his father had been in trade, and had no grandfather worth mentioning.

A few days after their return from Hadleigh, there was another long business interview with Mr. Trinder, in which everything was settled. A tenant had already been found for the cottage. A young couple, on the eve of their marriage, who had long been looking for a suitable house in the neighbourhood, had closed at once with Mr. Trinder's offer, and had taken the lease off their hands. The gentleman was a cousin of the Paines, and partly for the convenience of the in-coming tenants, and partly because the Challoners wished to move as soon as possible, there was only a delay of a few weeks before the actual flitting.

It would be impossible to describe the dismay of the neighbourhood when the news was circulated.

Immediately after their return from Hadleigh, Nan and Phillis took counsel together, and summoning up their courage, went from one to another of their friends, and quietly announced their approaching departure.

'Mother has had losses, and we are now dreadfully poor, and we are going to leave Glen Cottage and go down to a small house we have at Hadleigh,' said Nan, who by virtue of an additional year of age was spokeswoman on this occasion. She had fully rehearsed this little speech, which she intended to say at every house in due rotation. 'We will not disguise the truth; we will let people know that we are poor, and then they will not expect impossibilities,' she said, as they walked down the shady roads towards the Paines' house—for the Paines were their most intimate friends—and had a claim to the first confidence.

'I think that will be sufficient; no one has any right to know more,' she continued decidedly, fully determined that no amount of coaxing and cross-examination should wring from her one unnecessary word.

But she little knew how difficult it would be to keep their own counsel. The Paines were not alone—they very seldom were. Adelaide Sartoris was there, and the younger Miss Twentyman, and a young widow, a Mrs. Forbes, who was a distant connection of Mrs. Paine.

Nan was convinced that they had all been talking about them, for there was rather an embarrassed pause as she and Phillis entered the room. Carrie looked a little confused as she greeted them.

Nan sat down by Mrs. Paine, who was rather deaf, and in due time made her little speech. She was rather pale with the effort, and her voice faltered a little, but every word was heard at the other end of the room.

'Leave Glen Cottage, my dear? I can't have heard you rightly. 'I am very deaf, to-day, very. I think I must have caught cold,' and Mrs. Paine turned a mild face of perplexity on Nan, but, before she could reiterate her words Carrie was on the footstool at her feet, and Miss Sartoris, with a grave look of concern on her handsome features, was standing beside her.

'Oh, Nan! tell us all about it! Of course we saw something was the matter. Dulce was so strange that afternoon; and you have all been keeping yourselves invisible for ever so long.'

'There is very little to tell,' returned Nan, trying to speak cheerfully. 'Mother has had bad news. Mr. Gardiner is bankrupt, and all our invested money is gone. Of course, we could not go on living at Glen Cottage. There is some talk, Carrie, of your cousin, Mr. Ibbetson, coming to look at it; it will be nice for us if he could take the lease off our hands, and then we should go down to the Friary.'

'How I shall hate to see Ralph there; not but what it will suit him and Louisa well enough, I dare say. But never mind him, I want to know all about yourselves,' continued

Carrie affectionately. 'This is dreadful, Nan! I can hardly believe it. What are we to do without you? and where is the Friary? and what is it like? and what will you do with yourselves when you get there?'

'Yes, indeed, that is what we want to know,' agreed Miss Sartoris, putting her delicately gloved hand on Nan's shoulder; and then Sophy Paine joined the little group; and Mrs. Forbes and Miss Twentyman left off talking to Phillis, and began listening with all their might. Now it was that Nan began to foresee difficulties.

'The Friary is very small,' she went on, 'but it will just hold us and Dorothy. Dorothy is coming with us, of course. She is old, but she works better than some of the young ones. She is a faithful creature——'

But Carrie interrupted her impatiently:

'But, Nan, what will you do with yourselves? Hadleigh is a nice place, I believe. Mamma, we must all go down there next summer, and stay there—you shall come with us, Adelaide—and then we shall be able to cheer these poor things up; and, Nan, you and Phillis must come and stay with us.

We don't mean to give you up like this. What does it matter about being poor? We are all old friends together. You shall give us tea at the Friary; and I dare say there are tennis grounds at Hadleigh, and we will have nice times together.'

'Of course we will come and see you,' added Miss Sartoris, with a friendly pressure of Nan's shoulder; but the poor girl only coloured up and looked embarrassed, and then it was that Phillis, who was watching her opportunity, struck in.

'You are all very good; but, Carrie, I don't believe you understand Nan one bit. When people lose their money they have to work. We shall all have to put our shoulder to the wheel. We would give you tea, of course, but as for paying visits and playing tennis, it is only idle girls like yourselves who have time for that sort of thing. It will be work and not play, I fear, with us.'

'Oh, Phillis!' exclaimed poor Carrie, with tears in her eyes, and Miss Sartoris looked horrified, for she had West Indian blood in her veins, and was by nature somewhat indolent and pleasure-loving.

'Do you mean you will have to be governesses?' she asked, with a touch of dismay in her voice.

'We shall have to work,' returned Phillis vaguely. 'When we are settled at the Friary we must look round us and do the best we can.' This was felt to be vague by the whole party; but Phillis's manner was so bold and well assured that no one suspected that anything lay beyond the margin of her speech. They had not made up their minds, perhaps —Sir Francis Challoner would assist them; or there were other sources of help; they must move into the new house first, and then see what was to be done. It was so plausible, so sensible that everyone was deceived.

'Of course, you cannot decide in such a hurry; you must have so much to do just now,' observed Carrie. 'You must write and tell us all your plans, Phillis, and if there be anything we can do to help you. Mamma, we might have Mrs. Challoner here while the cottage is dismantled. Do spare her to us, Nan, and we will take such care of her!' and they were still discussing this point, and trying to overrule Nan's objections—who knew nothing would induce her mother to leave them—when other visitors were announced, and in the confusion they were allowed to make their escape.

## CHAPTER XII.

'LADDIE' PUTS IN AN APPEARANCE.

'I THINK we have managed that as well as possible!' exclaimed Phillis, when they found themselves outside the gates. 'What a good thing Adelaide and Mrs. Forbes and Lily were there! Now we need only call at those three houses to say good-bye. How hot you look, Nan! and how they all hemmed you in! I was obliged to come to your rescue, you were so beset; but I think I have put them off the scent.'

'Yes, for the present; but think, Phil, if Carrie really carries out her intention, and all the Paine tribe and Adelaide come down to Hadleigh next summer! No wonder I am hot; the bare idea suffocates me.'

'Something may turn up before then; it is no good looking so far ahead,' was the philosophical rejoinder. 'Adelaide is rather formidable certainly, and, in spite of her good nature, one does not feel at home with her. There is a flavour of money about her, I think; she dresses, talks, and lives in such a gilded way one finds her heavy; but she may get married before then. Mr. Dalrymple certainly seemed to mean it when he was down here last winter, and he will be a good match for her; but here we are at Fitzroy Square. I wonder what sort of humour her ladyship will be in?'

Lady Fitzroy received them very graciously. She had just been indulging in a slight dispute with her husband, and the interruption was welcome to both of them; besides, she was always gracious to the Challoners.

'You have just come in time, for we were boring each other dreadfully,' she said, in her pretty languid way, holding out a hand to each of them. 'Percival, will you ring the bell, please? I cannot think why Thorpe does not bring up the tea "as usual"?'

Lord Fitzroy obeyed his wife's behest obediently; and then he turned with a relieved air to his old friend Phillis. She was the clever one; and though some people called her quiet, that was because they did not draw her out, or she had no sympathy with them. He had always found her decidedly amusing and agreeable in the days of his bachelorhood.

He had married the beauty of a season, but the beauty was not without her little crotchets and tempers; and though he was both fond and proud of his wife, he found Phillis's talk a relief this afternoon.

But Phillis was a little *distraite* on this occasion; she wanted to hear what Nan was saying in a low voice across the room, and Thorpe and his subordinate was setting the tea-table, and Lord Fitzroy would place himself just before her.

'Now look here, Miss Challoner,' he was saying, ' I want to tell you all about it;' but here Thorpe left the room, and Lady Fitzroy interrupted them.

' Oh, Percival, what a pity! Do you hear we are going to lose our nicest neighbours?

Dear little Glen Cottage is to be empty in a week or so!'

'Mr. Ralph Ibbetson will decide to take it, I think; and he and Miss Blake are to be married on the sixteenth of next month,' returned Nan softly.

'Ibbetson at Glen Cottage! that red-headed fellow! My dear Miss Challoner, what sacrilege—what desecration! What do you mean by forsaking us in this fashion? Are you all going to be married? Has Sir Francis died and left you a fortune? In the name of all that is mysterious, what is the meaning of this?'

'If you will let a person speak, Percival,' returned his wife with dignity, 'you shall have an answer;' and then she looked up in his handsome, good-natured face, and her manner softened insensibly. 'Poor dear Mrs. Challoner has had losses! Some one has played her false, and they are obliged to leave Glen Cottage. But Hadleigh is a nice place,' she went on, turning to Nan; 'it is very select.'

'Where did you say, Evelyn?' inquired her husband, eagerly. 'Hadleigh, in Sussex?

Oh, that is a snug little place; no Toms and Harries go down there on a nine hours' trip. I was there myself once, with the Shannontons. Perhaps Lady Fitzroy and I may run down one day and have a look at you,' he continued, with a friendly look at Phillis. It was only one of his good-natured speeches, but his wife took umbrage at it.

'The sea never agrees with me. I thought you knew that, Percival!' rather reproachfully; 'but I dare say we shall often see you here,' she went on, fearing Nan would think her ungracious. 'You and the Paines are so intimate that they are sure to have you for weeks together; it is so pleasant revisiting an old neighbourhood, is it not? I know I always feel that with regard to Nuneaton.'

'Nuneaton never suits my constitution. I thought you would have remembered that, Evelyn,' returned her husband gravely; and then they both laughed. Lord Fitzroy was not without a sense of humour, and often restored amity by a joking word after this fashion, and then the conversation proceeded more smoothly.

Nan and Phillis felt far more at their ease

here than they had at the Paines'. There were no awkward questions asked; Lady Fitzroy was far too well bred for that. If she wondered at all how the Challoners were to live after they had lost their money, she kept such remarks for her husband's private ear.

'Those girls ought to marry well,' observed Lord Fitzroy, when he found himself alone again with his wife. 'Miss Challoner is as pretty a creature as one need see, but Miss Phillis has the most in her.'

'How are they to meet people if they are going to bury themselves in a little seaside place?' she returned regretfully. 'Shall I put on my habit now, Percy? do you think it will be cool enough for our ride?'

'Yes, run along, my pet, and don't keep me too long waiting.' Nevertheless, Lord Fitzroy did not object when his wife made room for him a moment beside her on the couch, while she made it up to him for her cross speeches, as she told him.

'There, little mother, it is all done!' exclaimed Phillis, in a tone of triumph, as later on in the afternoon they returned to the cottage; but in spite of her bravado both the girls looked terribly jaded, and Nan especially seemed out of spirits; but then they had been round the Longmead garden, and had gathered some flowers in the conservatory, and this alone would have been depressing work to Nan.

From that time they lived in a perpetual whirl, a bustle of activity that grew greater, and not less, from day to day. Mrs. Challoner had quietly but decidedly refused the Paines' invitation. Nan was right, nothing would have induced her to leave her girls in their trouble: she made light of their discomfort, forgot her invalid airs, and persisted in fatiguing herself to an alarming extent.

'You must let me do things; I should be wretched to sit with my hands before me and not help you,' she said, with tears in her eyes, and when they appealed in desperation to Dorothy, she took her mistress's side.

'Working hurts less than worrying. Don't you be fretting about the mistress too much, or watching her too closely. It will do her no harm, take my word for it;' and Dorothy was right.

But there was one piece of work that Nan set her mother to do before they left the cottage.

'Mother,' she said to her one day when they were alone together, ' Mrs. Mayne will be wondering why you do not answer her letter. I think you had better write, and tell her a little about things. We must not put it off any longer, or she will be hurt with us;' and Mrs. Challoner very reluctantly set about her unpleasant task.

But after all it was Nan who furnished the greater part of the composition. Mrs. Challoner was rather verbose and descriptive in her style. Nan cut down her sentences ruthlessly; and so penned and simplified the whole epistle, that her mother failed to trace her own handiwork; and at the last she added a postscript in her own pretty handwriting.

Mrs. Challoner was rather dissatisfied with the whole thing.

' You have said so little, Nan. Mrs. Mayne will be quite affronted at our reticence.'

'What is the use of harrowing people's feelings?' was Nan's response.

It was quite true she had dwelt as little as possible on their troubles.

The few opening sentences had related solely to their friends' affairs.

'You will be sorry to hear,' Mrs. Challoner wrote after this, ' that I have met with some severe losses. I dare say Mr. Mayne will remember that my poor husband invested our little income in the business of his cousin, Mark Gardiner. We have just heard the unwelcome news that Gardiner and Fowler have failed for a large amount. Under these circumstances, we think it more prudent to leave Glen Cottage as soon as possible, and settle at Hadleigh, where we have a small house belonging to us called the Friary. Fortunately for us Mr. Trinder has found us a tenant, who will take the remainder of the lease off our hands. Do you remember Mr. Ralph Ibbetson, the Paines' cousin, that rather heavy-looking young man with reddish hair, who was engaged to that pretty Miss Blake—well, he has taken Glen Cottage; and I hope you will find them nice neighbours. Tell Dick he must not be too sorry to miss his old friends; but of course you will understand this is a sad break to us. Settling down in a new place is never very pleasant; and as my girls will have to help themselves, and we shall all have to learn to do without things, it will be somewhat of a discipline to us; but as long as we are together, we all feel such difficulties can be easily borne.

'Tell Mr. Mayne that if I had foreseen how things were to turn out, I would have conquered my indisposition, and not have forfeited my last evening at Longmead.'

And in the postscript Nan wrote hurriedly:

'You must not be too sorry for us, dear Mrs. Mayne, for mother is as brave as possible, and we are all determined to make the best of things.

'Of course, it is very sad leaving dear Glen Cottage, where we have spent such happy, happy days; but though the Friary is small, we shall make it very comfortable. Tell Dick the garden is a perfect wilderness at present, and that there are no roses, only a splendid passion-flower that covers the whole back of the house.'

Nan never knew why she put this. Was it to remind him vaguely that the time of roses was over, and that from this day things would be different with them.

Nan was quite satisfied when she had despatched this letter. It told just enough, and not too much. It sorely perplexed and troubled Dick; and yet neither he nor his father had the least idea how things really were with the Challoners.

'Didn't I tell you so, Bessie?' exclaimed Mr. Mayne, almost in a voice of triumph, as he struck his hand upon the letter. 'Paine was right when he spoke of a shakey investment. That comes of women pretending to understand business. A pretty mess they seem to have made of it.'

'Mother,' said poor Dick, coming up to her when he found himself alone with her for a moment, 'I don't understand this letter. I cannot read between the lines, somehow, and yet there seems something more than meets the eye.'

'I am sure it is bad enough,' returned Mrs. Mayne, who had been quietly crying over Nan's postscript; 'think of them leaving Glen Cottage, and of these poor dear girls having to make themselves useful.'

'It is just that that bothers me so,' replied Dick, with a frowning brow. 'The letter tells us so little. It is so constrained in tone; as though they were keeping something from us. Of course they have something to live upon, but I am afraid it is very little.'

'Very likely they will only have one servant; just Dorothy, and no one else; and the girls will have to help in the house,' returned his mother thoughtfully. 'That will not do them any harm, Dick; it always improves girls to make them useful. I dare say the Friary is a very small place, and then I am sure, with a little help, Dorothy will do very well.'

'But, mother,' pleaded Dick, who was somewhat comforted by this sensible view of the matter, 'do write to Nan or Phillis, and beg of them to give us fuller particulars,' and, though Mrs. Mayne promised she would do so, and kept her word, Dick was not satisfied, but sat down and scrawled a long letter to Mrs. Challoner, so incoherent in its expressions of sympathy and regret, that it quite mystified her; but Nan thought it perfect, and took possession of it, and read it every day, until it got quite thin and worn. One sentence especially pleased her. 'I don't intend ever to cross the threshold of the Cottage again,' wrote Dick; 'in fact, Oldfield will be hateful without you all. Of course I shall run down to Hadleigh at Christmas, and look you up, and see for myself what sort of a place the Friary is. Tell Nan I will get her lots of roses for her garden, so she need not trouble about that; and give them my love, and tell them how awfully sorry I am about it all.'

Poor Dick! the news of his friends' misfortunes took off the edge of his enjoyment for a long time. Thanks to Nan's unselfishness, he did not in the least realize the true state of affairs; nevertheless, his honest heart was heavy at the thought of the empty cottage, and he was quite right in saying Oldfield had grown suddenly hateful to him, and, though he kept these thoughts to himself as much as possible, Mr. Mayne saw that his son was depressed and ill at ease, and sent him away to the Swiss Tyrol, with a gay party of young people, hoping a few weeks' change would put the Challoners out of his head. Meanwhile, Nan and her sisters worked busily, and their friends crowded round them, helping or hindering, according to their nature.

On the last afternoon there was a regular invasion of the Cottage. The drawing-room carpet was up, and the room was full of packing-cases. Carrie Paine had taken possession of one, and her sister Sophy and Lily Twentyman had a turned-up box between them. Miss Sartoris and Gussie Scobell had wicker chairs. Dorothy had just brought in tea, and had placed before Nan a heterogeneous assemblage of kitchen cups and saucers, mugs, and odds and ends of crockery, when Lady Fitzroy entered in her habit, accompanied by her sister, the Honourable Maud Burgoyne, both of whom seemed to enjoy the picnic excessively.

'Do let me have the mug,' implored Miss Burgoyne; she was a pretty little brunette with a *nez retroussé*. 'I have never drank out of one since my nursery days. How cool it is, after the sunny roads. I think carpets ought to be abolished in the summer. When I have a house of my own, Evelyn, I mean to have Indian matting and nothing else in the warm weather.'

'I am very fond of Indian matting,' returned her sister, sipping her tea contentedly. 'Fitzroy hoped to have looked in this afternoon, Mrs. Challoner, to say good-bye, but there is an assault-at-arms at the Albert Hall, and he is taking my young brother Algernon to see it. He is quite inconsolable at the thought of losing such pleasant neighbours, and sent all sorts of pretty messages,' finished Lady Fitzroy graciously.

'Here is Edgar,' exclaimed Carrie Paine; 'he told us at lunch-time that he meant to put in an appearance; but I am afraid the poor boy will find himself *de trop* among so many ladies.'

Edgar was the youngest Paine. A tall Eton boy, who looked as though he would soon be too big for jackets, and an especial friend of Nan's.

'How good of you to come and say goodbye, Gar,' she said, summoning him to her side, as the boy looked round him blushing and half terrified. 'What have you got there under your jacket?'

'It is the puppy I promised you,' returned Edgar eagerly; 'don't you know, Nell's puppy? Father said I might have it,' and he deposited a fat black retriever puppy at Nan's feet. The little beast made a clumsy rush at her, and then rolled over on its back. Nan took it up in high delight, and showed it to her mother.

'Isn't it good of Gar, mother, and when we all wanted a dog so? We have never had a pet since poor old Juno died, and this will be such a splendid fellow when he grows up; look at his head and curly black paws, and what a dear solemn face he has got.'

'I am glad you like him,' replied Edgar, who was now perfectly at his ease; 'we have christened him "Laddie," he is the handsomest puppy of the lot, and our man Jakes says he is perfectly healthy,' and then, as Nan cut him some cake, he proceeded to enlighten her on the treatment of this valuable animal.

The arrival of 'Laddie' made quite a diversion, and when the good-byes were all said, Nan took the little animal in her arms and went with Phillis for the last time to gather flowers in the Longmead garden, and when the twilight came on the three girls went slowly through the village, bidding farewell to their old haunts.

It was all very sad, and nobody slept much that night in the cottage. Nan's tears were shed very quietly, but they fell thick and fast.

'Oh, Dick, it is hard—hard!' thought the poor girl, burying her face in the pillow; 'but I have not let you know the day, so you will not be thinking of us. I would not pain you for worlds, Dick, not more than I can help,' and then she dried her eyes and told herself that she must be brave for all their sakes to-morrow, but for all her good resolutions sleep would not come to her any more than it did to Phillis, who lay open-eyed and miserable until morning.

## CHAPTER XIII.

'I MUST HAVE GRACE.'

WHEN the Rev. Archibald Drummond was nominated to the living of Hadleigh in Sussex, it was at once understood by his family that he had achieved a decided success in life.

Hadleigh until very recently had been a perpetual curacy, and the perpetual curate in charge had lived in the large, shabby house with the green door on the Braidwood Road, as it was called. There had been some talk of a new vicarage, but as yet the first brick had not been laid, the building committee had fallen out on the question of the site, and nothing had been definitely arranged; there was a good deal of talk too about the church restoration, but at the present moment nothing had been done.

Mr. Drummond had not been disturbed in his mind by the delay of the building committee in the matter of the new vicarage, but on the topic of the church restoration he had been heard to say very bitter things, far too bitter, it was thought, to proceed from the lips of such a new comer. It is not always wise to be outspoken, and when Mr. Drummond expressed himself a little too frankly on the ugliness of the sacred edifice, which until lately had been a chapel-of-ease, he had caused a great deal of dissatisfaction in the mind of his hearers; but when the young vicar, still strongly imbued with the beauties of Oxford architecture, had looked round blankly on the great square pews and galleries, and then at the wooden pulpit, and the Ten Commandments that adorned the east end, he was not quite so sure in his mind that his position was as enviable as that of other men.

Church architecture was his hobby, and if the truth must be told he was a little ' High ' in his views ; without attaching himself to the

Ultra-Ritualistic party, he was still strongly impregnated with many of their ideas; he preferred Gregorian to Anglican chants, and would have had no objection to incense if his Diocesan could have been brought to have appreciated it too.

An ornate service was decidedly to his taste. It was, therefore, a severe mortification when he found himself compelled to minister Sunday after Sunday in a building that was ugly enough for a conventicle, and to listen to the florid voices of a mixed choir, instead of the orderly array of men and boys in white surplices, to which he had been accustomed. If he had been combative by nature—one who loved to gird his armour about him, and to plunge into every sort of mêlée, he would have rejoiced after a fashion at the thought of the work cut out for him, of bringing order and beauty out of this chaos; but he was by nature too impatient. He would have condemned and destroyed instead of trying to renovate.

'Why not build a new church at once?' he said, with a certain youthful intolerance that made people angry. 'Never mind the vicarage; the old house will last my time; but a place like this—a rising place—ought to have a church worthy of it. It will be money thrown away to restore this one,' finished the young vicar, looking round him with sorely troubled eyes; and it was this out-spoken frankness that had lost him popularity at first.

But if the new vicar had secret cause for discontent, in the Drummond family there was nothing but the sweetness of triumph.

'Archie has never given me a moment's trouble from his birth,' his proud mother was wont to declare; and it must be owned that the young man had done very fairly for himself.

There had been plenty of anxiety in the Drummond household while Archibald was enjoying his first Oxford term. Things had come to a climax—his father—who was a Leeds manufacturer, had failed most utterly, and to a large amount. The firm of Drummond and Drummond, once known as a most respectable and reliable firm, had come suddenly, but not unexpectedly, to the ground; and Archibald Drummond the elder had been compelled to accept a managership in the very firm who, by competition and under-selling, had helped to ruin him.

It was a heavy trial to a man of Mr. Drummond's proud temperament; but he went through with it in a tough, dogged way, that excited his wife's admiration. True, his bread was bitter to him for a long time, and the sweetness of life, as he told himself, was over for him; but he had a large family to maintain, sons and daughters growing up around him, and the youngest was not yet six months old; under such circumstances a man may be induced to put his pride in his pocket.

'Your father has grown quite grey, and has begun to stoop. It makes my heart quite ache to see him sometimes,' Mrs. Drummond wrote to her eldest son; 'but he never says a word to any of us. He just goes through with it day after day.'

At that time Archie was her great comfort. He had begun to make his own way early in life, understanding from the first that his parents could do very little for him. He had worked well at school, and had succeeded in obtaining one or two scholarships. When his university life commenced, and the household at Leeds became straitened in their circumstances, he determined not to encumber them with his presence.

He soon became known in his college as a reading-man and a steady worker; he was fortunate, too, in obtaining pupils for the long vacation. By-and-by he became a fellow and tutor of his college, and before he was eight-and-twenty the living of Hadleigh was offered to him. It was not at all a rich living—not being worth more than three hundred a year—and some of his Oxford friends would have dissuaded him from accepting it; but Archibald Drummond was not of their opinion. Oxford did not suit his constitution; he was never well there. Sussex air, and especially the seaside, would give him just the tone he required. He liked the big old-fashioned house that would be allotted to him. He could take pupils and add to his income in that way; at present he had his fellowship. It was only in the event of his marriage that his income might not be found sufficient. At the present moment he had no matrimonial intentions; there was only one thing on which he was determined, and that was, Grace must live with him and keep his house.

Grace was the sister next to him in age. Mattie, or Matilda, as her mother often called her, was the eldest of the family, and was two years older than Archibald. Between him and Grace there were two brothers, Fred and Clyde, and beyond Grace a string of girls, ending in Dottie, who was not yet ten. Archibald used to forget their ages, and mix them up in the most helpless way; he was never quite sure if Isabel were eighteen or twenty, or whether Clara or Susie came next. He once forgot Laura altogether, and was only reminded of her existence by the shock of surprise at seeing the awkward-looking, ungainly girl standing before him, looking shyly up in his face.

Archibald was never quite alive to the blessing of having seven sisters, none of them with any pretension to beauty, unless it were Grace, though he was obliged to confess on his last visit to Leeds that Isabel was certainly passable-looking. He tried to take a proper amount of interest in them, and be serenely unconscious of their want of grace and polish;

but the effort was too manifest, and neither Clara, nor Susie, nor Laura regarded their grave elder brother with any lively degree of affection. Mrs. Drummond was a somewhat stern and exacting mother, but she was never so difficult to please as when her eldest son was at home.

'Home is never so comfortable when Archie is in it,' Susie would grumble to her favourite confidante, Grace. 'Everyone is obliged to be on their best behaviour; and yet mother finds fault from morning to night. Dottie is crying now because she has been scolded for coming down to tea in a dirty pinafore.'

'Oh, hush, Susie dear, you ought not to say such things,' returned Grace, in her quiet voice.

Poor Grace! these visits of Archie were her only pleasures. The brother and sister were devoted to each other. In Archie's eyes not one of the others was to be compared to her; and in this he was perfectly right.

Grace Drummond was a tall, sweet-looking girl of two-and-twenty; not pretty, except in her brother's opinion, but possessing a soft, fair comeliness, that made her pleasant to look upon. In voice and manner she was extremely quiet—almost grave; and only those who lived with her had any idea of the repressed strength and energy of her character, and the almost masculine clearness of intellect that lay under the soft exterior. One side of her nature was hidden from everyone but her brother, and to him only revealed by intermittent flashes, and that was the passionate absorption of her affection in him. To her parents she was dutiful and submissive, but when she grew up the yoke of her mother's will was felt to be oppressive. Her father's nature was more in sympathy with her own; but even with him she was reticent. She was good to all her brothers and sisters, and especially devoted to Dottie; but her affection for them was so strongly pervaded by anxiety and the over-weight of responsibility, that its pains over-balanced its pleasures. She loved them, and toiled in their service from morning to night; but as yet she had not felt herself rewarded by any decided success. But in Archie her pride was equal to her love; she was critical, and her standard was somewhat high; but he satisfied her. What other people recognised as faults, she regarded as the merest blemishes. Without being absolutely faultless, which was of course impossible in a creature of flesh and blood, he was still as near perfection, she thought, as he could be. Perhaps her affection for him blinded her somewhat, and cast a sort of loving glamour over her eyes; for it must be owned Archibald was by no means extraordinary in either goodness or cleverness. From a boy she had watched his career with dazzled eyes, rejoicing in every stroke of success that came to him as though it were her own. Her own life was dull and laborious, spent in the over-crowded house in Lowder Street, but she forgot it in following his. Now and then bright days came to her—few in number, but absolutely golden—when this dearly loved brother came on a brief visit; when they had snatches of delicious talk in the empty schoolroom at the top of the house, or he took her out with him for a long quiet walk.

Mrs. Drummond always made some dry sarcastic remark when they came in, for she was secretly jealous of Archie's affection for

Grace. Hers was rather a monopolizing nature, and she would willingly have had the first share in her son's affections. It somewhat displeased her to see him so rapt up in the one sister to the exclusion of all the others, as she told him.

'I think you might have asked Matilda or Isabel to have accompanied you. The poor girls never see anything of you, Archie,' she would say plaintively to her son. But to Grace she would speak somewhat sharply, bidding her fulfil some neglected duty, which another could well have performed; and making her at once understand by her manner, that she was to blame in leaving Mattie at home.

'Mother,' Archibald said to her one day, when she had spoken with unusual severity, and the poor girl had retreated from the room, feeling as though she had been convicted of selfishness; 'we must settle the matter about which I spoke to you last night. I have been thinking about it ever since. Mattie will not do at all — I must have Grace!'

Mrs. Drummond looked up from her mending; and her thin lips settled into a hard line that they always took when her mind was made up on a disagreeable subject. She had a pinafore belonging to Dottie in her hand; there was a jagged rent in it; and she sighed impatiently as she put it down: though she was not a woman who shirked any of her maternal duties, she had often been heard to say that her work was never done, and that her mending basket was never empty.

'But if I cannot spare Grace,' she said rather shortly, as she meditated another lecture to the delinquent Dottie.

'But, mother, you must spare her!' returned her son eagerly, leaning his elbow on the mantelpiece, and watching her rapid manipulations with apparent interest. 'Look here, I am quite in earnest. I have set my heart on having Grace. She is just the one to manage a clergyman's household. She would be my right hand in the parish.'

'She is our right hand too, Archie; but I suppose we are to cut it off, that it may benefit you and your parish.'

Mrs. Drummond seldom spoke so sharply

to her eldest son ; but this request of his was grievous to her.

'I think Grace ought to be considered, too, in the matter,' he returned somewhat sullenly. 'She works harder than any paid governess, and gets small thanks for her trouble.'

'She does her duty,' returned Mrs. Drummond coldly—she very seldom praised any of her children—'but not more than Mattie does hers. You are prejudiced strangely against your sister, Archie; you are not fair to her in any way. Mattie is a capital little housekeeper. She is economical, and full of clever contrivances. It is not as though I asked you to try Isabel. She is well enough, too, in her way, but a little flighty, and rather too pretty perhaps——' but here a laugh from Archie grated on her ear.

'Too pretty!—what an absurd idea. The girl is passable-looking, and I will not deny that she has improved lately ; but, mother, there is not one of the girls that can be called pretty except Grace.'

Mrs. Drummond winced at her son's outspoken words. The plainness of her daughters was a sore subject.

She had never understood why her girls were so ordinary-looking. She had been a handsome girl in her time, and was still a fine-looking woman. Her husband, too, had had a fair amount of good looks; and though he stooped, was still admirable in her eyes. The boys, too, were thoroughly fine fellows. Fred was decidedly handsome, and so was Clyde; and as for her favourite Archie, Mrs. Drummond glanced up at him as he stood beside her.

He certainly looked a model young clergyman. His features were good, but the lower part of his face was quite hidden by the fair moustache and soft silky beard. He had thoughtful grey eyes, which could look as severe as hers sometimes; and though his shoulders were somewhat too sloping, there could be no fault found with his figure. He was as nice-looking as possible, she thought, and no mother could have been better satisfied. But why, with the exception of Grace and Isabel, were her girls so deficient in outward graces? It could not be denied that they were very ordinary girls. Laura was overgrown and freckled, and had red hair. Susie was sickly-looking, and so short-sighted that they feared she would have to take to spectacles; and Clara was stolid and heavy-looking, one of those thick-set girls that dress never seems to improve. Dottie had a funny little face; but one could not judge of her yet. And Mattie—Mrs. Drummond sighed again as she thought of her eldest daughter—Mattie was thirty; and her mother felt she would never marry. It was not that she was so absolutely plain—people who liked her said Mattie had a nice face—but she was so abrupt, so uncouth in her awkwardness, such a stranger to the minor morals of life, that it would be a wonder indeed if she could find favour in any man's eyes.

'I do think you are too hard on your sisters,' returned Mrs. Drummond, stung by her son's remark. 'Isabel was very much admired at her first party last week. Mrs. Cochrane told me so, and so did Miss Blair.' She could have added that her maternal interest had been strongly stirred by the mention of a certain Mr. Ellis Burton, who she had understood had paid a great deal of attention that evening to Isabel, and who was the eldest son of a wealthy manufacturer in Leeds. But Mrs. Drummond had some good old-fashioned notions, and one of these was never to speak on such delicate subjects as the matrimonial prospects of her daughters; indeed, she often thanked heaven she was not a match-making mother—which was as well, under the circumstances.

'Well, well, we are not talking about Isabel,' returned her son impatiently. 'The question is about Grace, mother. I really do wish very much that you and my father would stretch a point for me here. I want her more than I can say.'

'But, Archie, you must be reasonable. Just think a moment. Your father cannot afford to send the girls to school, or to pay for a good finishing governess. We have given Grace every advantage; and just as she is making herself really useful to me in the schoolroom, you want to deprive me of her services.'

'You know I offered to pay for Clara's schooling,' returned her son reproachfully. 'She is more than sixteen, is she not? Surely Mattie could teach the others?'

But Mrs. Drummond's clear, concise voice interrupted him.

'Archie, how can you talk such nonsense? You know poor Mattie was never good at book-learning. She would hardly do for Dottie. Ask Grace, if you doubt my word.'

'Of course I do not doubt it, mother,' in rather an aggravated voice, for he felt he was having the worst of the argument.

'Then why do you not believe me then, when I tell you the thing you ask is impossible?' replied his mother, more calmly. 'I am sorry for you if you are disappointed, Archie; but you undervalue Mattie—you do indeed. She will make you a nice little housekeeper, and though she is not clever, she is so amiable that nothing ever puts her out; and visiting the poor and sick-nursing are more in her line than in Grace's. Mrs. Blair finds her invaluable. She wanted her for one of her district visitors, and I said she had too much to do at home.'

Archie shrugged his shoulders. Mrs. Blair was the wife of the Vicar of All Saints', where the Drummonds attended, and from a boy she had been his pet aversion. She was a bustling, managing woman, and, of course, Mattie was just to her taste. He did not see much use in continuing the conversation; with all his affection for his mother—and she was better loved by her sons than by her daughters—he knew her to be as immovable as a rock when she had once made up her mind. He thought at first of appealing to his father on Grace's behalf, but abandoned this notion after a few minutes' reflection. His father was decided and firm in all matters relating to business, but for many years past he had abandoned the domestic reins to his wife's capable hands. Perhaps he had proved her worth and prudence; perhaps he thought the management of seven daughters too much for any man. Anyhow, he interfered less and less as the years went on; and if at any time he differed from his wife, she could always talk him over, as her son well knew.

When the subject had been first mooted in the household h had said a word or two to his father, and had found him very reluctant to entertain the idea of parting with Grace. She was his favourite daughter, and he thought how he should miss her when he came home weary and jaded at night.

'I don't think it will do at all,' he had said, in an undecided dissatisfied tone. 'Won't one of the other girls serve your turn? There's Mattie, or that little monkey Isabel, she is as pert and lively as possible. But Grace, why, she is everyone's right-hand. What would the mother or the young ones do without her?'

No; it was no use appealing to his father, Archie thought, and might only make mischief in the house. He and Grace must make up their mind to a few more years' separation. He turned away after his mother's last speech, and finally left the room without saying another word. There was a cloud on his face, and Mrs. Drummond saw that he was much displeased; but, though she sighed again as she took up a pair of Clyde's socks and inspected them carefully, there was no change in her resolution that Mattie, and not Grace, should go to the Vicarage for the year's visit that was all Archie had asked.

There are mothers and mothers in this

world. Some who are capable of sacrificing their children to Moloch, who will barter their own flesh and blood in return for some barren heritage or other. There are those who will exact from those dependent on them heavy tithes of daily patience and uncomplaining drudgery; while others, who are 'mothers indeed,' give all, asking for nothing in return.

Mrs. Drummond was a good woman. She had many virtues and few faults. She was ladylike, industrious, and self-denying in her own personal comforts, an exemplary wife and a tolerant mistress; but she was better understood by her sons than by her daughters.

Her maternal instincts were very strong, and no mother had more delighted in her nursery than she had in hers. As long as there was a baby in the house the tenderness of her love was apparent enough. She wore herself out tending her infants, and no one ever heard her say a harsh word in her nursery.

But as her children grew up, there was much clashing of wills in the household.

Her sons did not fear her in the least; but with her daughters it was otherwise. They felt the mother's strong will repressive; it threatened to dwarf their individuality, and cramp that free growth that is so necessary to young things.

Dottie, who by virtue of being the last baby had had more than her fair amount of petting, was only just beginning to learn her lesson of unquestioning obedience; and, as she was somewhat spoiled, the lesson was a hard one. But Laura, and Susie, and Clara had not yet found out that their mother loved them, and wished to be their friend; they were timid and reserved with her, and took all their troubles to Grace. Even Mattie, who was her first-born, and who was old enough to be her mother's companion, quailed and blushed like a child under the dry caustic speeches at which Clyde and Fred only laughed.

'You don't understand the mother. Her bark is worse than her bite,' Clyde would say to his sister sometimes. 'She is an awfully clever woman, and it riles her to see herself surrounded by such a set of ninnies. Now don't sulk, Belle. You know Mattie's a duffer compared to Grace; aren't you, Matt?'

At which truism poor Mattie would hang her head.

'Yes, Clyde; I know I am dreadfully stupid sometimes, and that makes mother angry.'

Mrs. Drummond often complained bitterly of her daughters' want of confidence in her, but she never blamed herself for the barrier that seemed between them. She was for ever asserting maternal authority, when such questions might have been safely laid to rest between her and her grown-up daughters. Mrs. Challoner's oneness of sympathy with her girls, her lax discipline, her perfect equality, would have shocked a woman of Mrs. Drummond's calibre. She would not have tolerated or understood it for a moment.

'My girls must do as I wish,' was a very ordinary speech in her mouth. 'I always do as my girls wish,' Mrs. Challoner would have said. And, indeed, the two mothers were utterly dissimilar; but it may be doubted whether the Challoner household were not far happier than the family in Lowder Street.

## CHAPTER XIV.

'YOU CAN DARE TO TELL ME THESE THINGS!'

ARCHIBALD DRUMMOND had left his mother's presence with a cloud on his brow. He had plenty of filial affection for her, but it was not the first time that he had found her too much for him. She had often angered him before by her treatment of Grace, but he had told himself that she was his mother, that a man could have but one, and so he had brought himself to forgive her. But this time she had set herself against the cherished plan of years. He had always looked forward to the time when he could have Grace to live with him; they had made all sorts of schemes together, and all their talk had concentrated itself towards this point; the disappointment would place a sort of blankness before them; they would be working separately, far away from each other, and the distance would not be bridged for years.

He stood for a moment in the dark, narrow hall, thinking intently over all this, and then he went slowly upstairs. He knew where he should find Grace. His mother had paid an unwonted visit to the schoolroom during their walk, and on their return had expressed herself with some degree of sharpness on the disorder she had found there. Grace would be busily engaged in putting everything to rights. It was Clara's business, but she had gone out, and had as usual forgotten all about it. Grace had taken the blame upon herself, of course; she was always shielding her younger sisters.

Everything was done when he entered the room, and Grace was sitting by the window, with her hands folded in her lap, indulging in a few minutes' rare idleness; she looked up eagerly as her brother made his appearance.

The schoolroom was a large, bare-looking room at the top of the house, with two narrow windows looking out over a lively prospect of roofs and chimney-pots. Mrs. Drummond had done her utmost to give it an air of comfort, but it was on the whole a dull, uncomfortable apartment, in spite of the faded Turkey carpet, and the curtains that had once been so handsome, but had now merged into unwholesome neutral tints.

Laura, who was the wit of the family, had nicknamed it the Hospital, for it seemed to be a receptable for all the maimed and rickety chairs of the household—footstools in a dilapidated condition, and odd pieces of lumber that had no other place. Archibald regarded it with a troubled gaze; somehow its dinginess had never so impressed him; and then as he looked at his sister the frown deepened on his face.

'Well, Archie.'

'Oh, Grace, it is no use! I have talked myself hoarse; but the mother is dead against it; one might as well try to move a rock. We shall have to make up our minds to bear our disappointment as well as we can.'

'I knew it was hopeless from the first,' returned Grace slowly; but as she spoke a sort of dimness and paleness crept over her face, belying her words.

She was young, and in youth hope never dies. Beyond the gray daily horizon there is always a possible gleam, a new to-morrow; youth abounds in infinite surprises, in probabilities which are as large as they are vague. Grace told herself that she never hoped much from Archie's mission; yet when he came to her with his ill-success plainly stamped upon his countenance, the dying out of her dream was bitter to her.

'I knew it was hopeless from the first,' had been her answer, and then breath for further words failed her; and she sat motionless, with her hands clasped tightly together, while Archie placed himself on the window-seat beside her, and looked out ruefully at the opposite chimneys.

Well, it was all over, this dearly cherished scheme of theirs; she must go on now with the dull routine of daily duties, she must stoop her neck afresh to the yoke she had long found so galling; this schoolroom must be her world, she must not hope any longer for wider vistas, for more expansive horizons, for tasks that should be more congenial to her, for all that was now made impossible.

Mattie, not she, must go and keep Archie's house, and here for a moment she closed her eyes, the pain was so bitter; she thought of the old vicarage, of the garden where she and Archie were to have worked, of the shabby old study where he meant to write his sermons, while she was to sit beside him with her book or needlework, of the evenings when he had promised to read to her, of the walks they were to have taken together, of all the dear delightful plans they had made.

And now her mother had said them nay; it was Mattie who was to be his housekeeper, who would sit opposite to him and pour out his coffee, who would mend his socks and do all the thousand and one things that a woman delights in doing for the mankind dependent on her for comfort.

Mattie would visit his poor people, and teach in the schools, entertain his friends, and listen to his voice every Sunday; here tears slowly gathered under the closed eyelids. Yes, Mattie would do all that, but she would not be his chosen friend and companion;

there would be no long charming talks for her in the study or the sunny garden, he would be as lonely, poor fellow, in his way as she would be in hers, and for this her mother was to blame.

'Well, Gracie, haven't you a word to say?' asked her brother at last, surprised at her long silence.

'No, Archie, it does not bear talking about,' she returned so passionately that he turned round to look at her. 'I must not even think of it. I must try and shut it all out of my mind, or I shall be no good to anyone. But it is hard—hard!' with a quiver of her lip.

'I call it a shame for my father and mother to sacrifice you in this way!' he burst out, moved to bitter indignation at the sight of her trouble. 'I shall tell my father what I think about it pretty plainly!'

But this speech recalled Grace to her senses.

'Oh no, dear! you must do no such thing —promise me you will not. It would be no good at all; and it would only make mother so angry. You know he always thinks as she does about things, so it would be no use. I suppose'—with an impatient sigh—' that I ought to feel myself complimented at knowing I cannot be spared. Some girls would be proud to feel themselves their mother's right hand; but to me it does not seem much of a privilege.'

'Don't talk in that way, Grace, it makes me miserable to hear you. I am more sorry for you than I am for myself, and yet I am sorry for myself too. If it were not that my mother would be too deeply offended, I would refuse to have Mattie at all. We never have got on well together. She is a good little thing in her way, but her awkwardness and left-handed ways will worry me incessantly. And then we have not an idea in common—' but here Grace generously interposed.

'Poor old fellow! as though I did not know all that; but you must not vent it on poor Mattie. She is not to blame for our disappointment. She would gladly give it up to me if she could. I know she will do her utmost to please you, Archie, and she is so good and amiable that you must overlook her little failings, and make the best of her.'

'It will be rather difficult work, I am afraid,' returned her brother grimly. 'I shall always be drawing invidious comparisons between you both, and thinking what you would do in her place.'

'All the same you must try and be good to her for my sake, for I am very fond of Mattie,' she returned gently; but she could not help feeling gratified at the assurance that he would miss her. And then she put her hand on his coat-sleeve, and stroked it—a favourite caress with her. 'It does not bear talking about—does it, Archie? It only makes it feel worse. I think it must be meant as a discipline for me, because I am so wicked; and that it would not do at all for me to be too happy;' and here she pressed his arm, and looked up in his face, with an attempt at a smile.

'No, you are right—talking only makes it worse,' he returned hurriedly; and then he stooped—for he was a tall man—and kissed her on the forehead, just between her eyes, and then walked to the door whistling a light air.

Grace did not think him at all abrupt in

thus breaking off the conversation. She had caught his meaning in a moment; and knew the whole business was so painful to him, that he did not care to dwell on it. When the tea-bell rang, she prepared herself at once to accompany him downstairs.

It was Archibald's last evening at home, and all the family were gathered round the long tea-table. Since Mr. Drummond's misfortunes, late dinners had been relinquished, and more homely habits prevailed in the household. Mrs. Drummond had indeed apologized to her son more than once for the simplicity of their mode of life.

'You are accustomed to a late dinner, Archie. I wished I could have managed it for you; but your father objects to any alteration being made in our usual habits.'

'He is quite right; and I should have been much distressed if you had thought such alteration necessary,' returned her son, very much surprised at this reference to his father. For Mrs. Drummond rarely consulted her husband on such matters. In this case, however, she had done so, and Mr. Drummond had been unusually testy, indeed, affronted at such a question being put to him.

'I don't know what you mean, Isabella,' he had replied; 'but I suppose what is good enough for me is good enough for Archie,' and then Mrs. Drummond knew she had made a mistake, for her husband had felt bitterly the loss of his late dinner. So Archie tried to fall in with the habits of his family, and to enjoy the large plum or seed-cake that invariably garnished the tea-table; and though he ate but sparingly of the supper, which always gave him indigestion, Grace was his only confidante in the matter. Mr. Drummond, indeed, looked at his son rather sharply once or twice, as though he suspected him of fastidiousness. 'I cannot compliment you on your appetite,' he would say as he helped himself to cold meat; 'but perhaps our home fare is not so tempting as Oxford living?'

'I always say your meat is unusually good,' returned Archibald amicably. 'If there be any fault it is in my appetite, but that Hadleigh air will soon set right.' But though he answered his father after this tolerant fashion, he always added in a mental aside, that nine o'clock suppers were certainly barbarous institutions, and peculiarly deleterious to the constitution of an Oxford fellow.

Mrs. Drummond looked at them both somewhat keenly as they entered. In spite of her resolution she was secretly uncomfortable at the thought that Archie was displeased with her; her daughter's vexation was a burden that could be more easily borne; but her maternal heart yearned for some token that her boy was not estranged from her. But no such consolation was to be vouchsafed to her. She had kept his usual place vacant beside her; Archie showed no intention of taking it. He placed himself by his father, and began talking to him of a change of Ministry that was impending, and which would overthrow the Conservative party. Mrs. Drummond, who was one of those women who could never be made to take any interest in politics, was reduced to the necessity of talking to Mattie in an undertone, for the other boys never put in an appearance at this meal; but as she talked, she took stock of Grace's pale, abstracted looks, as she sat with her plate before her, not pretending to eat, and taking no notice of Susie and Laura, who chatted busily across her.

It was not a festive meal; on the contrary, there was an unusual air of restraint over the whole party. The younger members felt instinctively that there was something amiss. Archie looked decidedly glum; and there was an expression on the mother's face that they were not slow to interpret. No one could hear what it was she was saying to Mattie that made her look so red and nervous all at once; but presently she addressed herself to her husband, breaking into his political discussion with more than her usual abruptness.

'It is all settled, father. I have arranged with Archie that Matilda should go down to Hadleigh next month.'

Archie stroked his beard, but did not look up or make any remark, though poor Mattie looked at him beseechingly across the table, as though imploring a word. His mother would carry her point; but he would not pretend for a moment that he was otherwise than displeased, or that Mattie would be welcome.

His silence attracted Mr. Drummond's attention.

'Oh, what, you have settled it, you say? I hope you are satisfied, Archie, and properly grateful to your mother for sparing Mattie. She is to go for a year. Well, it will be a grand change for her. I should not be surprised if you were to pick up a husband, Miss Mattie,' for Mr. Drummond was a man who, in spite of his cares, was not without his joke; but, as usual, it was instantly frowned down by his wife.

'I wonder at you, father, talking such nonsense before the children. Why are you giggling, Laura? It is very unseemly and ill-behaved. I hope no daughter of mine has such unmaidenly notions. Mattie is going to Hadleigh to be a comfort to her brother, and to keep his house as a clergyman's house ought to be kept.'

'And you are satisfied, Archie?' asked Mr. Drummond, not quite pleased at his wife's reprimand, and struck anew by his son's silence.

'I consider these questions somewhat unnecessary. You knew my wishes, sir, on the subject, and my mother also,' was the somewhat uncompromising remark; 'but it appears that they are not to be met in this instance. I hope Mattie will be comfortable and not miss her sisters,' but he did not look at the poor girl, and the tears came into her eyes.

'Oh, Archie! I am so sorry! I never meant——' she stammered, but her mother interrupted her.

'There is no occasion for you to be sorry about anything; you had far better be silent, Mattie. But you have no tact. Father, if you have finished your tea, I suppose you and Archie are going out,' and then Archie rose from the table and followed his father out of the room.

It was Isabel's business to put Dottie to bed. The other girls had to prepare their lessons for the next day, and went up to the schoolroom. Mattie made some excuse and went with them, and Mrs. Drummond and Grace were left alone.

Grace had some delicate work to finish, and she placed herself by the lamp. Her mother had returned to her mending basket;

but as the door closed upon Mattie she cleared her throat and looked at her daughter.

'Grace, I must say I am surprised at you!'

'Why, mother?' But Grace did not look up from the task she was running with such fine even stitches.

'I am more than surprised!' continued Mrs. Drummond severely. 'I am disappointed to see in what a bad spirit you have received my decision. I did not think a daughter of mine would have been so blind to her sense of duty.'

'I have said nothing to make you think that.'

'No, you have said nothing, but looks can be eloquent sometimes. I am not speaking of Archie, though I can see he is put out too, for he is a man, and men are not always reasonable; but that you should place yourself in such silent opposition to my wishes, it is that that shocks me.'

There was an ominous sparkle in Grace's gray eyes, and then she deliberately put down her work on the table. She had hoped that her mother would have been contented with her victory, and not have spoken to her on the subject, silence was so much safer between them. But if she were so attacked she would at least defend herself.

'You have no right to speak to me in this way, mother!'

'No right, Grace?' Mrs. Drummond could hardly believe her ears. Never once had a daughter of hers questioned her right in anything.

'No; for I have said nothing to bring all this upon me. I have been perfectly quiet, and have tried to bear the bitterness of my disappointment as well as I could. No one is answerable for their looks, and I, at least, will not plead guilty on that score.'

'Grace, you are answering me very improperly.'

'I cannot say that I think so, mother. I would have been silent, if you had permitted such silence; but when you drive me to speech, I must say what I feel to be the truth—that I have not been well treated in this matter.'

'Grace!' and Mrs. Drummond paused in awful silence. Never before had a recusant daughter braved her to her face.

'I have not been well treated,' continued Grace firmly, 'in a thing that concerns me more than anyone else. I have not even been consulted. You have arranged it all, mother, without reference to me or my feelings. Perhaps I ought to be grateful for being spared so painful a decision; but I think such a decision should have been permitted to me.'

'You can dare to tell me such things to my very face!'

'Why should I not tell them?' returned Grace, meeting her mother's angry glance unflinchingly. 'It seems to me that one should speak the truth to one's mother. You have treated me like a child; and I have a right to feel sore and indignant. Why did you not put the whole thing before me, and tell me that you and my father did not see how you could spare me? Do you really believe that I should have been so wanting in my sense of duty as to follow my own pleasure?'

'Grace, I insist upon your silence! I will not discuss the matter with you.'

'If you insist upon silence, you must be

obeyed, mother; but it is you who have raised the question between us. But when you attack me unjustly, I must defend myself.'

'You are forgetting yourself strangely. Your words are most disrespectful and unbecoming in a daughter. You tell me to my face that I am unjust—I, your mother—because I have been compelled to thwart your wishes.'

'No—no—not because of that!' returned Grace, in a voice of passionate pain. 'Why will you misunderstand me so!—but because you have no faith in me. You treat me like a child. You dispute my privilege to decide in a matter that concerns my own happiness. You bid me work for you, and you give me no wage—not a word of praise; and because I remonstrate for once in my life, you insist on my silence.'

'It seems that I am not to be obeyed.'

'Oh yes; you will be obeyed, mother. After to-night, I will not open my lips to offend you again. If I have said more than I ought to have said as a daughter, I will ask your pardon now; but I cannot take back one of my words. They are true—true!'

'I must say your apology is tardy, Grace.'

'Nevertheless it is an apology; for though you have hurt me, I must not forget you are my mother. I know my life will be harder after this, because of what I have said; and yet I would not take back one of my words!'

'I am more displeased with you than I can say,' returned her mother, taking up her neglected work; and her mouth looked stern and hard.

Never had her aspect been so forbidding, and yet never had her daughter feared her less.

'Then if you are displeased with me, I will go away,' replied Grace, moving from her seat with gentle dignity. 'I wish you had not compelled me to speak, mother, and then I should not have offended you; but as it is there is no help for it;' and then she gathered up her work, and walked slowly out of the room.

Mrs. Drummond sat moodily in the empty room that had somehow never seemed so empty before. Her attitude was as rigid and uncompromising as usual; but there was a perplexed frown on her brow. For the first time in her life one of her girls had dared to assert her own will, and to speak the truth to her; and she was utterly nonplussed. It was not too much to say that she had received a blow. Her justice and sense of fairness had been questioned — her very maternal authority impugned — and that by one of her own children! Mattie, who was eight years older, would not have ventured to cross her mother's will. Grace had so dared; and she was bitterly angry with her. And yet she had never so admired her before.

How honestly and bravely she had battled for her rights; her gray eyes had shone with fire; her pale cheeks had glowed with the passion of her words—for once in her life the girl had looked superbly handsome.

'You have no faith in me; you treat me like a child.' Well, she was right; it was no child, it was a proud woman who was flinging those hard words at her. For the first time Mrs. Drummond recognised the possibility of a will as strong as her own. In spite of all her authority, Grace had been a match for her mother—Mrs. Drummond knew this, and it added fuel to her bitterness.

'I know my life will be harder for what I have said.' Ah, Grace was right there; it would be long before her mother would forgive her for all those words, true as they were; and yet in her heart she had never so feared and admired her daughter. Grace went up to her own room, where Dottie was asleep in a little bed very near her sister's; it was dark and somewhat cold, but the atmosphere was less frigid than the parlour downstairs. Grace's frame was trembling with the force of her emotion; her face was burning, and her hands cold. It was restful and soothing to put down her aching head on the hard window-ledge and close her eyes and think out the pain! It seemed hours before Isabel came to summon her to supper, but she made an excuse that she was not hungry, and refused to go downstairs.

'But you ate nothing at tea, and your head is aching!' persisted Isabel, who was a bright, good-natured girl, and in spite of Archie's strictures decidedly pretty. 'Do let me bring you something. Mother will not know.'

But Grace refused—she could not eat, and the sight of food would distress her.

'Why not go to bed at once, then?' suggested Isabel, which was certainly sensible counsel. But Grace demurred to this; she knew Archie would be up presently to say good-night to her; so when Isabel had gone, she lighted the candle, shading it carefully from Dottie's eyes; and then she bathed her hot face, and smoothed her hair, and took up her work again.

Archie found her quite calm and busy, but he was not so easily deceived.

'Now, Gracie, you have got one of your headaches; it is the disappointment and the bother, and my going away to-morrow. Poor little Gracie!'

'Oh, Archie, I feel as though I shall never miss you so much!' exclaimed the poor girl, throwing down her work, and clinging to him. 'When shall I see your dear face again?—not until Christmas?'

'And not then, I expect. I shall most likely run down some time in January, and then I shall try hard to take you back with me just for a visit. Mattie will be dull, and wanting to see some of you, and I will not have one of the others until you have been.'

'I don't believe mother will spare me even for that,' returned Grace, with a sudden conviction that her mother's memory was retentive and that she would be punished in that way for her sins of this evening; 'but promise me, Archie, that you will come, if it be only for a few days.'

'Oh, I will promise you that, I cannot last longer without seeing you, Grace!' and he stroked her soft hair as she still clung to him.

The next day Archibald bade his family good-bye; his manner had not changed towards his mother, and Mrs. Drummond thought his kiss decidedly cold.

'You will be good to Mattie, and try to make the poor girl happy; you will do at least as much as this,' she said detaining him as he was turning from her to seek Grace.

'Oh yes, I will be good to her,' he returned indifferently, 'but I cannot promise that she will not find her life dull,' and then he took Grace in his arms and whispered to her to be patient, and that all would be well one day, and Mrs. Drummond, though she did not hear the whisper, saw the embrace and the long lingering look between the brother and sister, and pressed her thin lips together and went back to her parlour and mending-basket, feeling herself an unhappy mother, whose love was not requited by her children, and disposed to be harder than ever towards Grace, who had inflicted this pain on her.

## CHAPTER XV.

A VAN IN THE BRAIDWOOD ROAD.

ONE bright July morning, Mattie Drummond walked rapidly up the Braidwood Road, and unlatching the green door in the wall, let herself into the large square hall of the Vicarage. This morning it looked invitingly cool, with its summer matting and big wickerwork chairs; but Mattie was in too great haste to linger, she only stopped to disencumber herself of the various parcels with which she was laden, and then she knocked at the door of her brother's study, and without waiting for the reluctant 'come in' that always answered her hasty rap, burst in upon him.

It was now three months since Mattie had

entered upon her new duties, and it must be confessed that Archie's housekeeper had rather a hard time of it. As far as actual management went, Mattie fully justified her mother's eulogiums in her household arrangements: she was orderly and methodical, far more than Grace would have been in her place; the meals were always punctual and well served, the domestic machinery worked well and smoothly. Archie never had to complain of a missing button or a frayed wristband; nevertheless Mattie's presence at the Vicarage was felt by her brother as a sore burthen. There was nothing in common between them, nothing that he cared to discuss with her, or on which he wished to know her opinion; he was naturally a frank outspoken man, one that demanded sympathy from those belonging to him; but with Mattie he was reticent, and as far as possible restrained in speech.

One reason for this might be that Mattie, with all her virtues—and she was really a most estimable little person—was sadly deficient in tact. She never knew when she was treading on other people's pet prejudices. She could not be made to understand that her presence was not always wanted, and that it was as well to keep silence sometimes.

She would intrude her advice when it was not needed, in her good-natured way; she had always interfered with everything and everybody. 'Meddlesome Mattie' they had called her at home.

She was so wonderfully elastic, too, in her temperament, that nothing long depressed her. She took all her brother's snubbings in excellent part; if he scolded her at dinner-time, and made the ready tears come to her eyes —for it was not the least of Mattie's sins that she cried easily, and on every possible occasion—she had forgotten it by tea-time, and would chatter to him as happily as ever.

She was just one of those persevering people who seem bound to be snubbed; one could not help it. It was as natural to scold Mattie as it was to praise other people; and yet it was impossible not to like the little woman, though she had no fine feelings, as Archie said, and was not thin-skinned. Grace always spoke a good word for her— she was very kind to Mattie in her way— though it must be owned that she showed her small respect as an elder sister. None of her brothers and sisters respected Mattie in the least; they laughed at her, and took liberties with her, presuming largely on her good-nature. 'It is only Mattie; nobody cares what she thinks,' as Clyde would often say. 'Matt the Muddler,' as Frederick named her.

'I wonder what Mattie would say if any-one ever fell in love with her?' Grace once observed in fun to Archie. 'Do you know, I think she would be all her life thanking her husband for the unexpected honour he had done her, and trying to prove to him that he had not made such a great mistake after all.'

'Mattie's husband! He must be an odd sort of person, I should think,' and then Archie laughed, in not the politest manner. Certainly Mattie was not appreciated by her family. She was not looking her best this morning when she went into her brother's study. She wore the offending plaid dress; a particular large black and white check that he thought especially ugly. Her hat-trim-mings were frayed, and the straw itself was burnt brown by the sun, and her hair was ill-arranged and rough, for she never wasted much time on her own person, and to crown the whole, she looked flushed and heated.

Archie, who was sitting at his writing-table in severely cut ecclesiastical garments, looking as trim and well-appointed a young clergyman as one might wish to see, might be forgiven for the tone of ill-suppressed irritation with which he said:

'Oh, Mattie! what a figure you look! I am positively ashamed that anyone should see you. That hat is only fit to frighten the birds.'

'Oh, it will do very well for the mornings,' returned Mattie, perfectly undisturbed at these compliments. 'Nobody looks at me, so what does it matter?' But this remark, which she made in all simplicity, only irritated him more.

'If you have no proper pride, you might at least consider my feelings. Do you think a man in my position likes his sister to go about like an old beggar-woman? You are enough to try anyone's patience, Mattie, you are, indeed!'

'Oh, never mind me and my things,'

returned Mattie coaxingly; 'and don't go on writing just yet,' for Archie had taken up his pen again with a great show of being busy. 'I want to tell you something that I know will interest you. There are some new people come to the Friary.'

'What on earth do you mean?—what Friary? I am sure I never heard of such a place.'

'Dear me, Archie, how cross you are this morning,' observed Mattie in a cheerful voice, as she fidgeted the papers on the table. 'Why, the Friary is that shabby little cottage just above us—not a stone's throw from this house.'

'Indeed! Well, I cannot say I am much interested in the movements of my neighbours. I am not a gossip like you, Mattie!' —another fling at poor Mattie. 'I wish you would leave those papers alone. You know I never allow my things to be tidied, as you call it, and I am really very busy just now. I am in the middle of accounts, and I have to write to Grace, and——'

'Well, I thought you would like to know,' and Mattie looked rather crestfallen and disappointed. 'You talked so much about those young ladies some weeks ago, and seemed quite sorry not to see them again; and now—' but here Archie's indifference vanished, and he looked up eagerly.

'What young ladies—not those in Milner's Library, who asked about the dressmaker?'

'The very same,' returned his sister, delighted at this change of manner. 'Oh, I have so much to tell you that I must sit down,' planting herself comfortably on the arm of an easy-chair near him. Another time Archie would have rebuked her for her unladylike attitude, and told her probably that Grace never did such things; but now his interest was so excited that he let it pass for once. He even suffered her to take off her old hat and deposit it unreproved on the top of his cherished papers. 'I was over at Crump's this morning, to speak to Bobbie about weeding the garden, when I was surprised to see a railway van unloading furniture at the Friary.'

'What an absurd name!' *sotto voce* from Archie; but he offered no further check to Mattie's gossip.

'I asked Mrs. Crump, as a matter of course, the name of the new people; and she said it was Challoner. There was a mother and three daughters, she believed. She had seen two of them—pretty nice-spoken young creatures, and quite ladies. They had been down before to see the cottage, and to have it done up. It looks quite a different place already — nicely painted, and the shrubs trimmed. The door was open, and as I stood at Mrs. Crump's window—peeping between her geraniums—I saw such a respectable gray-haired woman, like an upper servant, carrying something into the house; and a moment after one of those young ladies we saw in the Library—not the pretty one, but the other—came to the door and spoke to the men.'

'Are you sure you did not make a mistake, Mattie?' asked her brother incredulously. 'You are very short-sighted—perhaps you did not see correctly. How can those stylish-looking girls live in such a shabby place? I can hardly believe it possible.'

'Oh, it was the same—I am positive about that. She was in the same cambric dress you admired. I could see distinctly. I watched her for a long time; and then the pretty one came out and joined her. She is pretty, Archie—she has such a lovely complexion.'

'But are they poor?—they don't look so. What on earth can it mean?' he asked, in a perplexed voice; but Mattie only shook her head, and went on:

'We must find out all about them by-and-by. They are worth knowing, I am sure of that. Poor?—well, they cannot be rich, certainly, to live in the Friary; but they are gentlepeople, one can see that in a moment.'

'Of course! who doubted it?' was the somewhat impatient answer.

'Well, but that is not all,' went on Mattie, too delighted with her brother's interest to try to curtail her story. 'Of course I could not stand long watching them, so I did my errand and came away; and then I met Miss Middleton, and we walked down to the library together to change those books. Miss Milner was talking to some ladies when we first went in, and as Miss Masham was not in the shop, we had to wait our turn, so I had a good look at them. The elder one was such a pretty, aristocratic-looking woman—a little too languid, perhaps, for my taste; and the younger one was a little like Isabel, only nicer looking. I shouldn't have stared at them so much—at least, I am afraid I stared,' went on Mattie, forgetting for the moment how often she had been taken to task for this very thing—'but something Miss Milner said attracted my attention. "I am not to send it to the Friary then, ma'am?" "Well, no," the lady returned, rather hesitatingly. She had such a nice voice and manner, Archie. "My youngest daughter and I are at Beach House at present; I am rather an invalid, and the bustle would be too much for me. Dulce, we had better have these things sent to Beach House." And then the young lady standing by her said: "Oh yes, mother, we shall want them this evening." And then they went out.'

'There is a third sister, then?' observed Archie, not pretending to disguise his interest in Mattie's recital.

'Yes, there is a third one; she is certainly a little like Isabel; she has a dimple like hers, and is of the same height. I asked Miss Milner, when they were out of hearing, if their name were Challoner, and if they were the new people who were coming to live at the empty cottage on the Braidwood Road. I thought she did not seem much disposed to give me information. Yes, their name was Challoner, and they had taken the Friary; but they were quite strangers in the town, and no one knew anything about them. And then Miss Middleton chimed in; she said her father had noticed the young ladies some weeks ago, and had called her attention to them. They were very pretty girls, and had quite taken his fancy; he had not forgotten them, and had spoken of them that very morning. She supposed Mrs. Challoner must be a widow, and not very well off—did Miss Milner know. Would you believe it, Archie? Miss Milner got quite red, and looked confused. You know how she enjoys a bit of gossip generally; but the questions seemed to trouble her. "They were not at all well off; she knew that, but nicer young ladies she had never seen, or wished to see; and she hoped everyone would be kind to them, and not forget they were real-born ladies, in spite of——" and here the old thing got more confused than ever, and came to a full stop, and begged to know how she could serve us.'

'It is very strange—very strange indeed,' returned her brother, in a meditative voice; but as Mattie had nothing more to tell him, he did not discuss the matter any further, only thanked her for her news, and civilly dismissed her on the plea that his business was at a standstill.

But he did not resume his accounts for some time after he was left alone. Instead of doing so, he walked to the window, and looked out in a singularly absent manner. Mattie's news was somewhat exciting. The idea of having such pleasant neighbours located within a stone's throw of the Vicarage was in itself disturbing to the imagination of a young man of eight-and-twenty, even though a clergyman. And then it must be confessed Nan's charming face and figure had never been forgotten; he had looked out for the sisters many times since his chance encounter with Phillis, and had been secretly disappointed at their total disappearance. And now they proved not mere visitors, but positively inhabitants of Hadleigh. He would meet them every day; and as there was but one church in the place, they would of course be numbered amongst his flock. As their future clergyman he would have a right of entrance to the cottage.

'How soon do you think we ought to call upon them, Mattie?' he asked, when he was seated opposite to his sister at the luncheon table. The accounts had not progressed very favourably, and the letter to Grace was not yet commenced. Mattie's news had been a sad interruption to his morning's work.

'Whom do you mean, Archie?' she returned, a little bewildered at this abrupt remark; and then, as he frowned at her denseness, she bethought herself of the new people. It was not often Archie asked her advice about anything, but on this occasion the young Vicar felt himself incompetent to decide.

'I suppose you mean the new folk at the Friary,' she continued carelessly. 'Oh, they are only moving in to-day, and they will be in a muddle for a week, I should think. I don't think we can intrude for ten days or so.'

'Not if you think it will be intrusive,' he returned rather anxiously; 'but they are strangers in the place, and all ladies—there does not seem to be a man belonging to them—would it not be neighbourly, as we live so close, just to call, not in a formal way, you know, but just to volunteer help? There are little things you could do for them, Mattie; and, as a clergyman, they could not regard my visit as an intrusion, I should think. Do you not agree with me?' looking at his sister rather gravely.

'Well, I don't know,' replied Mattie bluntly; 'I should not care for strangers prying into my concerns, if I were in their place. And yet, as you say, we are such close neighbours, and one would like to be kind to the poor things, for they must be lonely, settling in a strange new place. I'll tell you what, Archie,' as his face fell at this matter-of-fact speech, 'it is Thursday, and they will be sure to be at church on Sunday; we shall see them there, and that will be an excuse for us to call on Monday. We can say then that we are neighbours, and that we would not wait until they were all in order. We can offer to send them things from the Vicarage, or volunteer help in many little ways. I think that would be best.'

'Yes, perhaps you are right, and we will wait until Monday,' returned Archie, taking up his soft felt hat. 'Now I must go on my rounds, and not waste any more time chattering.' But though he spoke with unusual good-nature, he did not invite Mattie to be his companion, and the poor little woman betook herself to the solitary drawing-room and some plain sewing for the rest of the afternoon.

The young clergyman stood for a moment irresolutely at the green door, and cast a longing glance in the direction of the Friary, where the van was still unloading, and then he bethought himself that though Mattie had given orders about the weeding of the garden-paths, it would be as well to speak to Crump about the wire fence that was wanted for the poultry-yard; and as soon as he had made up his mind on this point, he walked on briskly.

The last piece of furniture had just been carried in; but, as Mr. Drummond was picking his way through the straw and débris that littered the side-path, two girlish figures came out of the doorway full upon him.

He raised his hat involuntarily, but they drew back at once; and, as he went out, confused at this sudden rencontre, the sound of a light laugh greeted his ear.

'How annoying that we should always be meeting him!' observed Nan innocently. 'Don't laugh, Phillis; he will hear you.'

'My dear, it must be fate,' returned Phillis solemnly. 'I shall think it my duty to warn Dick if this goes on.' But in spite of her mischievous speech she darted a quick, interested look after the handsome young clergyman as he walked on. Both the girls stood in the porch for some minutes after they had made their retreat. They had come out to cool themselves and to get a breath of air, until a July sun and Mr. Drummond's sudden appearance defeated their intention. They had no idea that they were watched from behind the screening geraniums in Mrs. Crump's window; both of them were enveloped in Dorothy's bib-aprons, which hid their pretty rounded figures. Phillis's cheeks were flushed, and her arms were bare to the dimpled elbows; and Nan's brown hair was slightly dishevelled.

'We look just like cooks!' exclaimed Phillis, regarding her coarse apron with disfavour; but Nan stretched her arms with a little indifference and weariness.

'What does it matter how we look—like cooks or housemaids? I am dreadfully tired; but we must go in and work, Phil. I wonder what has become of Dulce?' And then the charming vision disappeared from the young clergyman's eyes, and he was free to fix his mind on the wire fence that was required for the poultry-yard.

As soon as he had accomplished his errand he set his face towards the Vicarage, for he made up his mind suddenly that he would call on the Middletons, and perhaps on Mrs. Cheyne. The latter was a duty that he owed to his pastoral conscience; but there was no need for him to go to the Middletons. Nevertheless, the father and daughter were his most intimate friends, and on all occasions he was sure of Miss Middleton's sympathy. They lived at Brooklyn—a low white house a little below the Vicarage. It was a charming house, he always thought, so well arranged and well managed; and the garden—that was the Colonel's special hobby—was as pretty as a garden could be. The drawing-room looked shady and comfortable, for the French windows opened into a cool veranda, fitted up with flower-baskets and wicker-chairs; and beyond lay the trim lawn, with beds of blazing verbenas and calceolarias. Miss Middleton's work-table was just within one of the windows; but the Colonel, in his grey summer suit, reclined in a lounging-chair in the veranda. He was reading the paper to his daughter, and was just in the middle of last night's debate; nevertheless, he threw it aside, well pleased at the interruption.

'I knew how I should find you occupied,' observed Mr. Drummond, as he exchanged a smile with Miss Middleton. He was fully aware that politics were not to her taste, and yet every afternoon she listened to such reading, well content even with the sound of her father's voice.

Elizabeth Middleton was certainly a charming person. Phillis had called her the 'gray-haired girl,' and the title suited her. She was not a girl by any means, having reached her six-and-thirtieth year; but her hair was as silvery as an old woman's, gray and plentiful, and soft as silk, and contrasted strangely with her still youthful face.

Without being handsome, Elizabeth Middleton was beautiful. Her expression was sweet and restful, and attracted all hearts. People who were acquainted with her said she was the happiest creature they knew— that she simply diffused sunshine by her mere presence; such a contrast, they would add, to her neighbour, Mrs. Cheyne, who bore all her troubles badly, and was of a proud, fretful disposition. But then Mrs. Cheyne had lost her husband and her two children, and led such a sad, lonely life; and no such troubles had fallen to Miss Middleton.

Elizabeth Middleton could afford to be happy, they said, for she was the delight of her father's eyes. Her young half-brother, Hammond, who was with his regiment in India, was not nearly so dear to the old man; and of course that was why she had never married, that her father's house might not be left desolate.

This is how people talked; but not a single person in Hadleigh knew that Elizabeth Middleton had had a great sorrow in her life.

She had been engaged for some years most happily, and with her father's consent, to one of his brother officers. Captain Sedgwick was of good family, but poor; and they were waiting for his promotion, for at that time Colonel Middleton would have been unable to give his daughter any dowry. Elizabeth was young and happy, and she could afford to wait; no girl ever gloried in her lover more than she did in hers. Capel Sedgwick was not only brave and singularly handsome, but he bore a reputation through the whole regiment for having a higher standard of duty than most men.

Promotion came at last, and just as Elizabeth was gaily making preparations for her marriage, fatal tidings were brought to her. Major Sedgwick had gone to visit an old servant in the hospital who had been struck down with cholera; he had remained with him some time, and on his return to his bungalow the same fell disease had attacked him, and before many hours were over he was dead. The shock was a terrible one; in the first moments of her bitter loss, Elizabeth cried out that her misery was too great—that all happiness was over for her in this world, and that she only prayed that she might be buried in the same grave with Capel.

The light had not yet come to the poor soul that felt itself afflicted past endurance, and could find no reason for such pain. It could not be said that Elizabeth bore her trouble better than other girls would have borne theirs under like circumstances. She fretted and grew thin, and dashed herself wildly against the inevitable; only reproaching herself for her selfishness and want of submission when she looked at her father's careworn face.

But then came a time when light and peace revisited the wrecked heart—when confused reasonings no longer beset the poor weak brain, and filled it with dismay and doubt—when the Divine Will became her will; and there was no longer submission, but a most joyful surrender. And no one, and least of all she herself, knew when the darkness was vanquished by that clear uprising of pure radiance, or how those brooding wings of peace settled on her soul. From that time, every human being that came within her radius was welcome as a new object of love. To give, and yet to give, and never to be satisfied, was a daily necessity of life to Elizabeth. 'Now there is some one more to love,' she would say to herself, when a new acquaintance was brought to her; and, as the old adage is true that tells us love begets love, there was no more popular person in Hadleigh than Elizabeth Middleton. She had something to say in praise of everyone; not that she was blind to the faults of her neighbours, but she preferred to be silent, and ignore them.

And she was especially kind to Mattie. In the early days of their intimacy, the young Vicar would often speak to her of his sister Grace, and lament their enforced separation from each other. Miss Middleton listened sympathetically, with the same sweet attention that she gave to every man, woman, and child that laid claim to it; but once, when he had finished, she said rather gravely:

'Do you know, Mr. Drummond, that I think your mother was right?'

'Right in dooming Grace to such a life?' he said, pausing in utter surprise at her remark.

'Pardon me; it is not her mother who dooms her,' returned Miss Middleton quickly, 'but duty—her own sense of right—everything that is sacred. If Mrs. Drummond had not decided that she could not be spared, I am convinced, from all you tell me, that Grace would still have remained at home; her conscience would have been too strong for her.'

'Well, perhaps you are right,' he admitted reluctantly. 'Grace is a noble creature, and capable of any amount of self-sacrifice.'

'I am sure of it,' returned Miss Middleton, with sparkling eyes. 'How I should like to know her—it would be a real pleasure and privilege; but I am very fond of your sister Mattie, too.'

'Fond of Mattie!' it was hardly brotherly, but he could not help that incredulous tone in his voice. How could such a superior woman as Miss Middleton be even tolerant of Mattie?

'Oh yes,' she replied quite calmly; 'I have a great respect for your sister. She is so unselfish and amiable; and there is something so genuine in her. Before everything one wants truth,' finished Elizabeth, taking up her work.

Now, as the young clergyman entered the room, she stretched out her hand to him with her usual beaming smile.

'This is good of you to come so soon again,' she said, making room for him between her father and herself; 'but why have you not brought Mattie?' and Archie felt as though he had received a rebuke.

'She is finishing some work,' he returned, a little confused; 'that is, what you ladies call work. It is not always necessary for the clergywoman to pay visits, is it?'

'The clergywoman, as you call her, is doing too much. I was scolding her this morning for not sparing herself more; I thought she was not looking quite well, Mr. Drummond.'

'Oh, Mattie is well enough,' he replied carelessly. He had not come to talk about his sister—a far more interesting subject was in his mind. 'Do you know, Colonel,' he went on, with some animation, 'that you and I have new neighbours? Do you remember the young ladies in the blue cambric dresses?' and at this question the Colonel threw aside his paper at once.

'Elizabeth has been telling me. I remember the young ladies perfectly. I could not help noticing them. They walked so well—heads up, and as neat and trim as though they were on parade—pretty creatures, both of them. Elizabeth pretends not to be interested, but she is quite excited. Look at her!'

'Nay, father, it is you who can talk of nothing else; but it will be very nice to have such pleasant neighbours. How soon do you think we may call on them?'

And then Archie explained, with some little embarrassment, that he and Mattie thought of calling the following Monday, and offering their services.

'That is very thoughtful of Mattie. She

is such a kind-hearted little creature, and is always ready to serve everybody.'

And then they entered into a discussion on the new-comers that lasted so long that the tea-things made their appearance; and shortly afterwards Mr. Drummond announced that he must go and call on Mrs. Cheyne.

## CHAPTER XVI.

#### A VISIT TO THE WHITE HOUSE.

HITHERTO Mr. Drummond had acknowledged his afternoon to be a success. He had obtained a glimpse of the new-comers through Mrs. Crump's screen of geraniums, and had listened with much interest to Colonel Middleton's innocent gossip, while Miss Middleton had poured out their tea. Indeed, his attention had quite flattered his host.

'Really, Drummond is a very intelligent fellow,' he observed to his daughter, when they were at last left alone; 'a very intelligent fellow, and so thoroughly gentlemanly.'

'Yes, he is very nice,' returned Elizabeth; 'and he seems wonderfully interested in our new neighbours;' and here she smiled a little archly.

There was no doubt that Mr. Drummond had fully enjoyed his visit. Nevertheless, as he left Brooklyn, and set his face towards the White House, his manner changed, and his face became somewhat grave.

He had told himself that he owed it to his pastoral conscience to call on Mrs. Cheyne; but notwithstanding this monition, he disliked the duty, for he always felt on these occasions that he was hardly up to his office, and that this solitary member of his flock was not disposed to yield herself to his guidance. He was ready to pity her if she would allow herself to be pitied; but any expression of sympathy seemed repugnant to her. Anyone so utterly lonely, so absolutely without interest in existence, he had never seen or thought to see; and yet he could not bring himself to like her, or to say more than the mere commonplace utterances of society. Though he was her clergyman, and bound by the sacredness of his office to be specially tender to the bruised and maimed ones of his flock, he could not get her to acknowledge her maimed condition to him, or to do anything but listen to him with cold attention, when he hinted vaguely that all human beings are in need of sympathy. Perhaps she thought him too young, and feared to find his judgments immature and one-sided; but certainly his visits to the White House were failures. Mrs. Cheyne was still young enough and handsome enough to need some sort of chaperonage; and though she professed to mock at conventionality, she acknowledged its claims in this respect, by securing the permanent services of Miss Mewlstone—a lady of uncertain age, and uncertain acquirements.

It must be confessed that everyone wondered at Mrs. Cheyne and her choice, for no one could be less companionable than Miss Mewlstone.

She was a stout sleepy-looking woman, with a soft voice; and in placidity and a certain cosiness of exterior somewhat resembled a large white cat. Some people declared she absolutely purred; and certainly her small blue eyes were ready to close on all occasions. She always dressed in gray, a very unbecoming colour to a stout person; and when not asleep or reading, for she was a great reader, she seemed always busy with a mass of soft fleecy wool. No one heard her ever voluntarily conversing with her patroness. They would drive together for hours, or pass whole evenings in the same room, scarcely exchanging a word. 'Just so, my dear,' she would say, in return to any observation made to her by Mrs. Cheyne. 'Just-so-Mewlstone,' a young wag once nicknamed her.

People stared incredulously when Mrs. Cheyne assured them her companion was a very superior woman. They thought it was only her satire, and did not believe her in the least. They would have stared still more if they had really known the extent of Miss Mewlstone's acquirements.

'She seems so stupid, as though she cannot talk,' one of Mrs. Cheyne's friends said.

'Oh yes, she can talk, and very well too,' returned that lady quietly; 'but she knows that I do not care about it: her silence is her great virtue in my eyes. And then she has tact, and knows when to keep out of the way,' finished Mrs. Cheyne, with the utmost frankness; and, indeed, it may be doubted whether any other person would have retained her position so long at the White House.

Mrs. Cheyne was no favourite with the young pastor, nevertheless she was an exceedingly handsome woman. Before the bloom of her youth had worn off she had been considered absolutely beautiful. As regarded the form of her features, there was no fault to be found, but her expression was hardly pleasing. There was a hardness that people found a little repelling—a bitter, dissatisfied droop of the lip, a weariness of gloom in the dark eyes, and a tendency to satire in her speech, that alienated people's sympathy.

'I am unhappy, but pity me if you dare!' seemed to be written legibly upon her countenance; and those who knew her best held their peace in her presence, and then went away and spoke softly to each other of the life that seemed wasted and the heart that was so hardened with its trouble. 'What would the world be if everyone were to bear their sorrows so badly?' they would say; 'there is something heathenish in such utter want of resignation. Oh yes, it was very sad, her losing her husband and children, but it all happened four or five years ago, and you know,' and here people's voices dropped a little ominously, for there were vague hints afloat, 'that things had not always gone on smoothly at the White House, even when Mrs. Cheyne had her husband. She had been an only child, and had married the only survivor of a large family. Both were handsome, self-willed young people; neither had been used to contradiction. In spite of their love for each other, there was a strife of wills and misunderstandings from the earliest days of their marriage. Neither knew what giving up meant, and before many months were over the White House witnessed many painful scenes. Herbert Cheyne was passionate, and at times almost violent; but there was no malice in his nature. He stormed furiously and forgave easily. A little forbearance would have turned him into a sweet-natured man; but his wife's haughtiness and resentment lasted long; she never acknowledged herself in the wrong, never made overtures of peace, but bore herself on every occasion as a sorely injured wife, a state of things singularly provoking to a man of Herbert Cheyne's irritable temperament.

There was injudicious partizanship as regarded their children : while Mrs. Cheyne idolized her boy, her husband lavished most of his attentions on the baby girl; 'papa's girl,' as she always called herself in opposition to 'mother's boy.'

Mrs. Cheyne really believed she loved her boy best, but when diphtheria carried off her little Janie also, she was utterly inconsolable. Her husband was far away when it happened; he had been a great traveller before his marriage, and latterly his matrimonial relations with his wife had been so unsatisfactory that it had led to virtual separation. Two or three months before illness, and then death, had devastated the nursery at the White House he had set out for a long exploring expedition in Central Africa.

'You make my life so unbearable that, but for the children, I would never care to set foot in my home again,' he had said to her in one of his violent moods; and though he repented of this speech afterwards, she could not be brought to believe that he had not meant it, and her heart had been hard against him even in their parting.

But before many months were over she would have given all she possessed—to her very life—to have recalled him to her side. She was childless, and her health was broken, but no such recall was possible. Vague rumours reached her of some miserable disaster; people talked of a missing Englishman. One of the little party had already succumbed to fever and hardship, by-and-by another followed; the last news that reached them was that Herbert Cheyne lay at the point of death in the kraal of a friendly tribe. Since then the silence had been of the grave: not one of the party had survived to bring the news of his last moments; there had been illness and disaster from the first.

When Mrs. Cheyne recovered from the nervous disorder that had attacked her on the receipt of this news, she put on widow's mourning and wore it for two years; then she sent for Miss Mewlstone, and set herself to go through with the burthen of her life.

If she found it heavy she never complained; she was silent on her own as on other people's troubles. Only at the sight of a child of two or three years old she would turn pale and draw down her veil, and if it ran up to her, as would sometimes happen, she would put it away from her angrily, pushing it away almost with violence, and no child was ever suffered to cross her threshold.

The drawing-room at the White House was a spacious apartment with four long windows opening on the lawn. Mrs. Cheyne was sitting in her low chair reading, with Miss Mewlstone at the further end of the room, with her knitting-basket beside her; two or three greyhounds were grouped near her. They all rushed forward with furious barks as Mr. Drummond was announced, and then leaped joyously round him; Mrs. Cheyne put down her book and greeted him with a frosty smile.

She had laid aside her widow's weeds, but still dressed in black, the sombreness of her apparel harmonizing perfectly with her pale, creamy complexion. Her dress was always rich in material, and most carefully adjusted.

In her younger days it had been an art with her—almost a passion—and had grown into a matter of custom.

'You are very good to come again so soon, Mr. Drummond,' she said, as she gave him her hand. The words were civil; but a slight inflexion on the word 'soon' made Mr. Drummond feel a little uncomfortable. Did she think he called too often? He wished he had brought Mattie; only last time she had been so satirical, and had quizzed the poor little thing unmercifully; not that Mattie had found out that she was being quizzed.

'I hardly thought I should find you at home, it is so fine an afternoon; but I made the attempt, you see,' he continued, a little awkwardly.

'Your parochial conscience was uneasy, I suppose, because I was missing at church?' she returned somewhat slyly. 'You would make a capital overseer, Mr. Drummond'— with a short laugh. 'A headache is a good excuse, is it not? I had a headache, had I not, Miss Mewlstone?'

'Yes, my dear, just so,' returned Miss

Mewlstone. She always called her patroness 'my dear.'

'Miss Mewlstone gave me the heads of the sermon, so it was not quite labour lost, as regards one of your flock. I am afraid you think me a black sheep because I stay away so often — a very black sheep, eh, Mr. Drummond?'

'It is not for me to judge,' he said, still more awkwardly. 'Headaches are very fair excuses; and if one be not blessed with good health——'

'My health is perfect,' she returned, interrupting him ruthlessly. 'I have no such convenient plea under which to shelter myself. Miss Mewlstone suffers far more from headaches than I do. Don't you, Miss Mewlstone?'

'Just so; yes, indeed, my dear,' proceeded softly from the other end of the room.

'I am sorry to hear it,' commenced Mr. Drummond, in a sympathizing tone of voice. But his tormentor again interrupted him.

'I am a sad backslider, am I not? I wonder if you have a sermon ready for me?

Do you lecture your parishioners, Mr. Drummond, rich as well as poor? What a pity it is you are so young! Lectures are more suitable with gray hair; a hoary head might have some chance against my satire. A woman's tongue is a difficult thing to keep in order, is it not? I dare say you find that with Miss Mattie?'

Mr. Drummond was literally on thorns. He had no repartee ready. She was secretly exasperating him as usual, making his youth a reproach, and rendering it impossible for him to be his natural frank self with her. In her presence he was always at a disadvantage. She seemed to take stock of his learning, and to mock at the idea of his pastoral claims. It was not the first time she had called herself a black sheep, or had spoken of her scanty attendances at church. But as yet he had not dared to rebuke her; he had a feeling that she might fling back his rebuke with a jest, and his dignity forbade this. Some day he owed it to his conscience to speak a word to her—to tell her of the evil effects of such an example; but the convenient season had not yet arrived.

He was casting about in his own mind for some weighty sentence with which to answer her; but she again broke in upon his silence.

'It seems that I am to escape to-day. I hope you are not a lax disciplinarian; that comes of being young. Youth is more tolerant, they say, of other people's errors—they have their own glass houses to mind.'

'You are too clever for me, Mrs. Cheyne,' returned the young man, with a deprecating smile that might have disarmed her. 'No, I have not come to lecture—my mission is perfectly peaceful, as befits this lovely afternoon. I wonder what you ladies find to do all day?' he continued, abruptly changing the subject, and trying to find something that would not attract her satire.

Mrs. Cheyne seemed a little taken aback by this direct question; and then she drew up her beautiful head a little haughtily, and laughed.

'Ah, you are cunning, Mr. Drummond. You found me disposed to take the offensive in the matter of church-going, and now you are on another track. There is a lecture somewhere in the background. How doth the little busy bee, etc. Now don't frown'—as Mr. Drummond knitted his brows and really looked annoyed—'I will not refuse to be catechized.'

'I should not presume to catechize you,' he returned hastily. 'I appeal to Miss Mewlstone if my question were not a very innocent one.'

'Just so—just so,' replied Miss Mewlstone; but she looked a little alarmed at this appeal. 'Oh, very innocent—oh, very so.'

'With two against me I must yield,' returned Mrs. Cheyne, with a curl of her lip. 'What do we do with our time, Miss Mewlstone? Your occupation speaks for itself—it is exquisitely feminine. Don't tell Miss Mattie, Mr. Drummond, but I never work—I would as soon arm myself with a dagger as a needle or a pair of scissors. When I am not in the air, I paint—I only lay aside my palette for a book.'

'You paint!' exclaimed Archie, with sudden interest. It was the first piece of information he had yet gleaned.

'Yes,' she returned indifferently, 'one must do something to kill time, and music was never my forte. I sketch and draw and paint after my own sweet will. There are portfolios full of my sketches in there'—with a movement of her hand towards a curtained recess. 'No—I know what you are going to say—you will ask to see them; but I never show them to anyone.'

'For what purpose, then, do you paint them?' were the words on his lips; but he forbore to utter them. But she read the question in his eyes.

'Did I not say one must kill time?' she returned rather irritably; 'the occupation is soothing—surely that is reason enough.'

'It is a good enough reason, I suppose,' he replied reluctantly, for surely he must say a word here; 'but one need not talk about killing time with so much that one could do.'

Then there came a gleam of suppressed mischief in her eyes.

'Yes, I know—you may spare me that. I will listen to it all next Sunday if you will, when you have it your own way, and one cannot sin against decorum and answer you. Yes, yes—there is so much to do, is there not?—hungry people to be fed and sick to visit—all sorts of disagreeables that people call duties. Ah, I am a sad sinner! I only draw for my own amusement, and leave the poor old world to get on without me. What a burthen I must be on your conscience, Mr. Drummond—heavier than all the rest of your parish! What, are you going already? and Miss Mewlstone has never given you any tea.'

Then Archie explained very shortly that he had partaken of that beverage at Brooklyn, and his leave-taking was rather more formal than usual. He was very much surprised, as he stood at the hall-door, that always stood open in the summer, to hear the low sweep of a dress over the tesselated pavement behind him, and to see a white pudgy hand laid on his coat-sleeve.

'My dear Miss Mewlstone, how you startled me!'

'Just so—yes, I am afraid I did, Mr. Drummond; but I just wanted to say— never mind all that nonsense; come again, she likes to see you, she does, indeed. It is only her way to talk so; she means no harm, poor dear—oh, none at all!'

'Excuse me,' returned Archie, in a hurt voice, 'but I think you are mistaken. Mrs. Cheyne does not care for my visits, and shows me she does not; if it were not my duty I should not come so often.'

'No, no, just so; but all the same it rouses her and does her good. It is a bad day with her, poor dear! the very day the darlings were taken ill—four years ago. Now don't go away, and fancy things, don't, there's a dear young man; come as often as you can, and try and do her good.'

'Oh, if I only knew how that is to be done,' returned Archie slowly; but he was mollified in spite of himself. There were tears in Miss Mewlstone's little blue eyes; perhaps she was a good creature after all.

'I will come again; but not just yet,' he said, nodding to her good-humouredly; but as he walked down the road, he told himself that Mrs. Cheyne had never made herself so disagreeable, and that it would be long before he set foot in the White House again.

END OF VOL. I.

www.ingramcontent.com/pod-product-compliance
Lightning Source LLC
Chambersburg PA
CBHW030747230426
43667CB00007B/880